D0743732

# LEARNING TO
# LEAD

## WHAT *REALLY* WORKS FOR WOMEN IN LAW

Gindi Eckel Vincent, Author

Mary B. Cranston, Advisor

ABA
Defending Liberty
Pursuing Justice

Commission on Women
in the Profession
American Bar Association
**Celebrating 25 Years**

Cover design by Jill Tedhams/ABA Publishing.

The materials contained herein represent the opinions of the authors and/or the editors, and should not be construed to be the views or opinions of the law firms or companies with whom such persons are in partnership with, associated with, or employed by, nor of the American Bar Association or the ABA Commission on Women in the Profession unless adopted pursuant to the bylaws of the Association.

Nothing contained in this book is to be considered as the rendering of legal advice for specific cases, and readers are responsible for obtaining such advice from their own legal counsel. This book is intended for educational and informational purposes only.

Printed in the United States of America.

17 16 15 14 13  5 4 3 2

ISBN: 978-1-62722-214-3
Discounts are available for books ordered in bulk. Special consideration is given to state bars, CLE programs, and other bar-related organizations. Inquire at Book Publishing, ABA Publishing, American Bar Association, 321 N. Clark Street, Chicago, Illinois 60654-7598.

www.ShopABA.org

# The Commission on Women in the Profession

### Chair
Mary B. Cranston

### Members
Fred Alvarez
Ruthe Catolico Ashley
Hon. Fernande R.V. Duffly
Patricia Kruse Gillette
Carrie Hightman
Denise F. Keane
Jessica Kornberg
Paul W. Lee
Margaret K. Masunaga
Gloria Santona
Stephanie A. Scharf

### Staff
Shawn Taylor Kaminski, Director
Alia Graham
Barbara Leff
Beverly Tate
Melissa Wood

**American Bar Association Commission on Women in the Profession**
321 N. Clark Street, Chicago, Illinois 60654
Phone: 312-988-5715  Fax: 312-988-5790
E-mail: abacwp1@americanbar.org
Website: www.americanbar.org/women

*Any proceeds from this publication will go toward the projects
of the ABA Commission on Women in the Profession.*

# CONTENTS

# From the Chair of the ABA Commission on Women in the Profession

I have been most fortunate to have had a varied, interesting career as a practicing lawyer, a law firm managing partner, and a member of the boards of directors of prestigious corporations. I have seen first-hand many examples of highly successful women in both the legal profession and the business world. Through the work of the ABA Commission on Women in the Profession and my involvement with Catalyst, I have had the advantage of being exposed to the latest research in the field of leadership.

What I have learned for certain is that women *can* crack the glass ceiling. The path is there and can be replicated by women lawyers who want to reach the highest echelons. Twenty-five years ago, pioneer women business leaders and lawyers had to figure out what was effective by trial and error. Now we have a generation of robust research on which to draw. *Learning to Lead: What Really Works for Women in Law* provides a concise road map of that collective wisdom and the tools to become the best leader we can be.

It has been a privilege—and great fun—to work on this project under the auspices of the Commission, one of the foremost catalysts for change in the legal profession. The Commission is celebrating its 25th anniversary, and one of its highest priorities throughout the years has been to provide women lawyers with the information and tools they need to advance into leadership positions in all workplace environments within the law. Its programs, such as the Women in Law Leadership (WILL) Academy, help attendees identify the skills to enable them to be successful in business development, their organizations, and their communities in ways that will advance their careers to the next level. In addition, the Commission has produced numerous articles and publications on this critical subject, the latest being this book.

We owe an enormous debt of gratitude to author and long-time colleague Gindi Eckel Vincent, whose dedication, vision, and commitment helped to transform the idea for this publication into a reality. She culled through the research and has summarized in this book what I have seen and experienced in the past fifteen years. Deep thanks go to the eleven women leaders interviewed in chapters 6 and 7, who generously took the time to share their lessons learned and tips for successful leadership. Lastly, we appreciate and acknowledge the staff of the Commission and particularly our executive director, Shawn Taylor Kaminski, and the Commission's publications manager, Barbara Leff, who shepherded the book through production.

We hope you will be inspired to finish the book, take action, and chart your course to leadership and success.

—Mary B. Cranston, Chair, 2011–2013
ABA Commission on Women in the Profession

# Prologue

I have rows of books on my office bookshelves about (and by) women. The colors range from shocking pink to sober black. They all use action words in big, bold font. Each book in the stack shares insight into the gender divide. These books discuss important issues about why women don't run America's Fortune 500 companies, why women make 70 percent of men's salaries for comparable jobs, what holds women back from achieving their full potential, and a panoply of other pressing issues. I've even read most of them.

You could fill a train from the East Coast to the West Coast with the research done about gender inequality and what makes women successful. It is important research. These are important books.

This book, however, does not attempt to add another cargo load to that train. Instead, this book has three simple goals:

To synthesize and distill the research, anecdotal evidence, and key concepts on leadership techniques that help working women, in any field, develop in their careers.

To tailor these ideas and principles for women practicing law, regardless of practice area, and create practical actions that lawyers can implement in their lives and workplaces.

To recognize the uniqueness of what success and leadership look like for each individual woman practicing law and to put the learning into practice by hearing from women who are leading in legal fields, including the judiciary, and by seeing real-life transformations with a total leadership makeover.

First, much of the research and writing done identifies real issues that women face in male-dominated workplaces. While not every workplace fits that definition, many do. Even in workplaces that are incredibly progressive in dealing with gender inequality, there are clients or customers or opposing parties that do not share the same viewpoint. Additionally, there are deep-seated gender stereotypes, and what you are not aware of will hurt you. Identifying these stereotypes and ingrained behaviors is the best way to develop an action plan to combat them wherever you work today.

Second, many celebrated books on becoming a successful woman identify issues faced in particular careers. The takeaway action items are valuable but could be more impactful in a female lawyer's practice if tailored to some of the distinctive situations and challenges that confront women practicing law today. Identifying steps to take for building your network, taking risks, communicating with everyone you encounter, developing a reserve of energy, following your passion, and finding your highest and best use are key to becoming a recognized leader in your field and finding individualized success.

Finally, one of the stereotypes in the legal profession that has long been held, even by women, is that a successful leader in the profession fits into only one of a few boxes: The corporate executive. The managing partner. The Fortune 100 company board member. The president (of the United States or the ABA or any other widely recognized institution that hands out the title of president). Achieving one of those positions is not the only path to leadership in this noble profession. You can be the executive director of a nonprofit or legal aid organization. You can be a prosecutor. You can establish a reputable solo practice. You can be a respected part-time lawyer that juggles family, community, and the practice of law. You can lead a governmental agency's law department. You can also be the managing partner of an Am Law 100 firm or a corporate executive or the president. There are so many avenues to finding what works for you and then developing the critical leadership skills needed to be the best of the best in your field and your sphere of influence. This book has assembled some of the most impressive women leaders in the law today and leading female members of the judiciary to share advice that will move you to action as you see how they developed into remarkable leaders over the course of their careers. And then you can observe this advice being put into action as you see total leadership makeovers of real women lawyers unfold in the final pages.

This book is intentionally short. When you use words like *distill* and *practical* for an audience of working women, brevity is key. Hopefully, imparting the most useful nuggets of wisdom into a useable format will inspire you to: (a) finish the book, (b) take action, and (c) chart your course to leadership and success.

# Understanding the Lay of the Land

## The Statistics on Working and Leading Women

*Despite the encouraging and wonderful gains and the changes for women which have occurred in my lifetime, there is still room to advance and to promote correction of the remaining deficiencies and imbalances.*
— Sandra Day O'Connor, first female US Supreme Court justice

*The day will come when men will recognize woman as his peer, not only at the fireside, but in councils of the nation. Then, and not until then, will there be the perfect comradeship, the ideal union between the sexes that shall result in the highest development of the race.*
— Susan B. Anthony, American civil rights leader

■ ■ ■

At a bar association lunch recently, I sat next to a woman who has practiced law for over thirty years. She serves as a partner at a mid-sized regional law firm in an area of the country not known for overwhelmingly progressive law firms. We began discussing this book and its premise. The conversation remained with me for days. She remarked, "Women have it so easy now. Sure, there may not be a lot of women on corporate boards, but recently I heard there were TEN women CEOs of Fortune 100 companies. That's up from ZERO. And it's not just cosmetics. It's . . . Pepsi!"[1]

That sentiment clearly exists out there. Certainly much progress has been made over the past several decades for women to step into high-profile leadership opportunities. But there are two problems with that story line. First, gender equity is still a work in progress. The gap is narrowing, but inequalities still have to be tackled. Second, there is a definite need to equip women with the skills they need to lead that are completely unrelated to what the national or global statistics of women in leadership show. Regardless of whether that means demonstrating leadership skills as the go-to solo practitioner in your area or leading Google as its CEO, leadership is a finely honed and critical skill that leads to greater success and satisfaction.

This is not a book about gender issues; this is a book about leadership. Although we will touch briefly on the current workforce, this book focuses on how to help you lead and what obstacles you may need to identify in order to overcome them. These beneficial techniques will advance your career regardless of whether there are 100 or 100,000 women leaders in America. While there may always be room for improvement in promoting women in certain fields, the ability of a woman to identify and develop her leadership strengths and then apply them to her career will only improve our profession as a whole and you as an individual.

## WOMEN IN THE NATIONAL WORKFORCE

First, what does the US workforce look like? It may help to understand a bit of the history. In 1964, 19 million of the country's nonfarm employees were women. By 2010, over 65 million women had jobs, and 66.7 percent of those women had either attended college or graduated with a degree. That means that women accounted for 46.7 percent of the labor force by 2008.[2] The 2009 statistics published in 2011 by the US Department of Labor's Bureau of Labor Statistics (BLS) showed that 59 percent of working-age women in the United States were in the labor force. There are only a few countries in the world that have higher rates of female participation rates in the labor force. The BLS predicts that the number of women in the civilian labor force will continue to grow through 2020.[3] In addition to the dramatic changes happening in the diversity of fields and occupations within that statistic, there also are dramatic changes in the types of women entering the labor force. Today most mothers, even those with very young children, participate in the labor force.[4]

Dramatic changes do not appear only in the workforce, but also in the pipe-line: education. Women have been earning more bachelor's degrees than men since 1982 and more master's degrees than men since 1981. Women were esti-mated to earn 59 percent of all postsecondary degrees conferred in 2008.[5] Despite the advances in education and job opportunities, salaries have not kept pace. According to the BLS, the ratio of women's to men's earnings, for all occu-pations, was 81.2 percent.[6]

There is also an overarching challenge in attaining high-level leadership for women. Even though women make up about half of America's labor force, only eighteen Fortune 500 companies, and an additional twenty-one Fortune 501–1000 companies, have women CEOs or presidents.[7] Catalyst, the leading nonprofit membership organization expanding opportunities for women and business and a source of much information about women in the workplace (and law) today, points out that its data show little change over the last ten years. In 1998, 11 percent of corporate officers in Fortune 500 companies were women. This percentage rose to a peak of 16 percent by 2005 but has since fallen, although the 2012 Fortune 500 numbers are encouraging. While this is progress, Catalyst notes that, at this rate, it would take forty years for the number of female corpo-rate officers to match the number of male officers.[8]

Even politics shows no more promise than the modern-day corporate board-room. Women held 98, or about 18 percent, of the 535 seats in the 113th US Con-gress, 20 of the 100 seats in the Senate, and 78 of the 435 seats in the House of Representatives. The state-level political leadership opportunities for women fare somewhat better: in 2012, 73 women held statewide elective executive offices across the country—23 percent of the 320 available state executive positions.[9]

## WOMEN IN LAW

While law firms do not suffer the fate of Fortune 500 companies when compar-ing the percentage of women in leadership, there is still a dramatic step change between the number of women getting out of law school and those women rising to the top in a variety of legal fields and practices. Women comprised only 3.7 percent of law students in 1963, but they made up 44 percent of the student body by the 2007–2008 school year. Yet, the *ABA Journal* reported in June 2012 that only fifty law firms, out of all of the law firms in the country that employ more than a hundred lawyers, achieved the "gold standard" for putting women in leadership positions, as ranked by the Women in Law Empowerment Forum.[10] The year before, only thirty-two firms made the list. Among the six criteria required to qualify are that women account for at least 20 percent of equity partners and women represent at least 10 percent of the top half of the most highly compensated partners. But even that gold standard says that the best in show is a 20 percent female equity partnership when nearly half of the law school student body is female. In a survey of the fifty best law firms for women, the numbers reveal a striking challenge in gender equality: 10 percent of firm chairpersons were women, 12 percent of the firms had women managing partners, and 19 percent of the equity partners were women.[11]

While the percentages of women and men graduating from law school are within several points, more substantial changes quickly occur from that jumping off point:

- Women make up 33 percent of all lawyers, 45 percent of law firm associates, and 47 percent of JD students.
- Women constitute about 20 percent of partners in law firms.
  - Of the largest law firms in the United States, 11 percent have no women on their governing committees.
  - Women partners constituted only 16 percent of those partners receiving credit for having $500,000 worth of business or more.
- A recent study revealed that no state has ever achieved equality of women and men in federal or state judgeships and that only 22 percent of all federal judgeships are held by women and, similarly, only 27 percent of state judgeships are held by women.
- Approximately just over 20 percent of law school deans are women.
- Of the top legal officers at Fortune 500 companies in 2011, 108 were women.
- Women lawyers made not quite 87 percent of men lawyers' weekly salaries in 2011. [12]

One of the underlying interesting statistics, the implications of which will be explored, is that nearly half as many men lawyers as women lawyers (44 percent vs. 84 percent) have a spouse that is employed full-time.[13] That means the marketplace is not seeing a surge in stay-at-home dads, even now, though we continue to see stay-at-home wives and mothers supporting their lawyering husbands. That can translate to women not having the same support system or flexibility available to them in order to be able to work late hours and jump into emergency projects if they have family obligations. Given the same rate of change that the numbers above reflect, Catalyst estimates that it will take more than a current woman lawyer's lifetime to achieve equality.

It may be daunting to slog through all these numbers. Statistics do not tend to make the *New York Times* best-seller list. However, knowing the lay of the land is important in understanding the environment in which we practice and what obstacles could occur as a result.

## WHAT THIS MEANS FOR LEADERSHIP

What do any of these numbers mean when it comes to leadership? Obviously, you can have a talent for leadership and not serve as justice on the US Supreme Court or as general counsel for a Fortune 100 company. However, the statistics do show that there is a gender divide that can impede maximizing leadership potential. In a searing article aimed at changing legal culture, Anne-Marie Slaughter, former Harvard law professor and director of policy planning at the State Department, concludes that women can't have it all with the way the current American economy and legal culture are structured.[14]

American Bar Association President Laurel G. Bellows (2012–2013) highlighted the glass ceiling that still exists in the law with her Task Force on Gender Equity. Bellows pointed out that there has been no change to the mere 16 percent of women equity partners in the top 200 law firms in America in almost ten years. Bellows writes,

> Although women have made great strides in law and in society as a whole, they remain grossly underrepresented in positions of power, influence and leadership. For example, did you know that despite the fact that close to half of law students are now women and more than half of judicial clerks are women, the percentage of women equity partners has remained static at 16 percent or less? Did you know that, according to our latest statistics, 85 percent of women of color left large firms after five years? There are many reasons that the glass ceiling continues to limit women's progress, including implicit bias and hidden stereotypes. . . . We have come a long way. But we cannot stop now. We have much more to do before our law firms operate at full capacity by reaping the benefits that each of us can contribute—regardless of gender.[15]

American Bar Association President Wm. T. (Bill) Robinson III (2011–2012) also identified issues confronting women serving in the legal profession as their careers progress, and he encouraged change: "The underrepresentation of women in law firm leadership positions and the disparity in compensation have contributed to the high rate of attrition of women from the profession. Other factors are law firms' inflexibility with billable-hour quotas, stigmatization of part-time and flex-time programs, and unequal treatment of women in allocating credit for business development."[16]

Much progress has been made. There are many more strides still to take. These numbers do highlight unique challenges women lawyers may face in not only learning to lead despite fewer high-level female mentors but also becoming recognized leaders in their own right. However, leadership is a personal journey. Because you must develop your own brand of leadership regardless of the fluctuating statistics of women in traditional leadership roles, it is critical, for *YOUR* journey, to learn the keys to leadership and apply them in your daily sphere of influence. But first, you need to know what mountain you will be climbing. So let's explore the landscape of myths and stereotypes.

# 2

# The Men, The Myths, The Legends

## Understanding Myths and Stereotypes

*The king was in his countinghouse counting out his money;*
*The queen was in the parlor eating bread and honey.*
—"Sing a Song of Sixpence"

*I hate to hear you talk about all women as if they were fine ladies instead of*
*rational creatures. None of us want to be in calm waters all our lives.*
—Jane Austen, *Persuasion*

■ ■ ■

One of the greatest roadblocks to leading successfully is lack of knowledge. There are myths and stereotypes held by society in general about women in leadership, but *you* can also unknowingly hold misconceptions about what it takes to become a leader in the workforce. While the studies and findings on gender stereotypes are interesting and informational (the appendices contain more details on these findings), none of them are dispositive. In fact, some even contradict each other. Becoming aware of potential myths or stereotypes that you may be confronted with equips you to ask the right questions. Do you personally believe one or more of these myths? Are there people in the workplace around you who hold some stereotypes that could impede your ability to succeed as a leader in your career and community? If so, understanding misperceptions and unconscious bias arms you with the knowledge to combat them. Then disregard the principles inapplicable to you or your work situation. Raising awareness, whether that is self-awareness or workplace awareness, of the myths or stereo-types that hinder your ability to become a recognized leader in your field will enable you to overcome them.

## WHAT ARE THE MYTHS?

There are mountains of articles on myth-busting for women leaders. One article that highlights most of the key findings that various authors have made about myths and stereotypes is *7 Myths about Getting Ahead—What Women Need to Know*. The seven myths are as follows:

- Women need to model men's strategies to succeed.
- Women can't be assertive.
- You have to do it all—all by yourself.
- You have to lose who you are to what you do.
- If you work hard enough, you'll get noticed.
- Being good is good enough.
- If you don't do it yourself, it won't be done right.[17]

Do you see a theme? Solo, solo, solo. You, you, you. You have to do it, you have to sacrifice, you have to be good and work hard. In the next chapter, we will unpack what the research says actually works, but recognize that if you are hold-ing on to a notion that reinforces the idea that you work in a silo or have to alter who you are, then you will have some roadblocks to move out of the way before you head down leadership lane.

Does this issue resonate with any of you Type A readers? Women are great multitaskers. But that often means we aren't great delegators. It's easy to think, *Oh, what's one more thing on the pile?* One of the women we interviewed for this book laughingly highlighted a rather obvious point: *To be a leader, you have to have followers.*

If you are going to lead well, then you have to delegate. You have to network. You have to connect up and down the chain of command and outside it. But many leadership myths trip us up. *I really could do a better job myself, so I will just tackle this one thing. Plus, then everyone will see what a hard worker I am. Also, I really have to do it all myself because bringing in others is just a show of weakness.* This "I" myth only works to eliminate a myriad of career and leadership opportunities from your reach. You must build a team. You must have supporters. You must be capable of managing others well. You must be able to communicate your message of action so someone other than you can effectively execute it. By hanging on to internal myths, you reduce your opportunities and your potential.

What other myths does this story line reinforce? It reinforces that just doing a good job will provide you the opportunity for new challenges and leadership roles. It will not. The ability to share your successful story line and history of exceptional performance is a critical component in leading and succeeding It reinforces that you can't be you to get ahead. Finally, an internal focus can negate a natural skill set. For example, women are often more intrinsically capable and comfortable with collaboration and teamwork. Developing a collaborative environment where you delegate tasks to a team can showcase your strengths and highlight your leadership talent. If that is not a natural talent you possess, then it is time to begin developing that skill set.

Furthermore, as women we often struggle with being intensely self-critical. One judge interviewed noted that women attorneys would come to her incredibly upset about a courtroom loss and questioning every choice they made whereas their male counterparts were far more likely to attribute the loss to the jury or forces beyond their control. It is critical to reframe the voice in your head into one with a positive perspective rather than one that furthers the myth that everything that goes wrong is your fault. Whatever the story line is internally, you must take charge of it. There are a number of voices that reinforce negative or myth-inducing beliefs that you have to identify and redirect. If you hear a voice that says, *Well, I'm doing a good job, so I'll just keep my head down and someone will notice me and reward me,* then you must redirect it to say, *I'm doing a great job on this project, so I need to highlight my contribution to the partner in charge or the division leader and ask to be considered for the promotion coming available in the spring.* If you hear a voice that says, *I'm really not as good as the other members on this team, and I'm sure the case would have been won if I had argued more persuasively*, then you need to redirect it to say, *Boy, that was a hard loss, but I've learned more about that judge and understanding what the jury hears versus what I say, so I will incorporate that into my next victory.* The story line in your head all too often informs the reality in your life, so take it in hand and begin your work toward overcoming the myths that greatness requires timidity, long suffering, inauthenticity, or overloading yourself.

## WHAT ARE THE STEREOTYPES (AND ARE THEY DIFFERENT)?

But even more than the myths that speak through the voices in our head, stereotypes held by people around us and in society can stymie opportunities for women to lead. A stereotype is defined as a conventional, formulaic, and oversimplified conception, opinion, or image. As a result of the many changes in business with women serving as leaders, there is no shortage of stereotypes in the American workplace. One of the preeminent studies on stereotypes of US business leaders conducted by Catalyst, entitled "Women 'Take Care,' Men 'Take Charge,'" notes: [18]

> Countless stories in the popular press reinforce misperceptions of women leaders by speculating about how they are different from men. These stories "sell" because they resonate with popular beliefs about women and men. Although provocative, the stories are dangerous. They reinforce perceptions that are dead wrong—perceptions that are rooted in gender stereotypes—perceptions that maintain the gender gap in leadership itself. These stereotypic beliefs spill over into the workplace, posing an invisible and powerful threat to women leaders. Gender stereotypes portray women as lacking the very qualities that people commonly associate with effective leadership. As a result, they often create false perceptions that women leaders just don't measure up to men in important ways.[19]

The study identified an interesting twist in gender stereotypes: Both male and female leaders considered women to be superior to men at "take care" behaviors such as supporting and rewarding others but considered men superior to women at "take charge" behaviors such as delegating and influencing upward. Executives in the study were asked about their perceptions of women's and men's leadership *behavior*.[20]

The study found that another key to overcoming certain gender stereotypes is changing how the genders view women's problem solving skill set. Women said that more women were better at problem solving than men, but men respondents said that men were superior to women in problem-solving effectiveness. Catalyst showed that because men far outnumber women in top management positions, that male perspective—that women are poor problem-solvers—dominates corporate thinking. Being known as an effective problem-solver is crucial because it is a trait most commonly associated with successful leaders. Thus, women find themselves in a predicament: Because the stereotype causes people to lose faith in women's problem-solving competence, they may be reluctant to follow the direction of women leaders, and with their problem-solving skills undermined, women lose interpersonal power. As a result, women may have to rely on their status or position to influence others instead of using their credibility or expertise (which may be difficult, as women make up only 15 percent–16 percent of Fortune 500 corporate officers).[21]

What is so interesting about stereotypes and these extensive research exercises is that the final study often finds that facts directly contradict the beliefs. For example, Caliper, a Princeton-based management consulting firm, and Aurora, a London-based organization that works to advance women, conducted a yearlong study that identified a number of characteristics that distinguish women leaders from men when it comes to qualities of leadership. The researchers found that women leaders are more persuasive than their male counterparts; learn from adversity and carry on with an "I'll show you" attitude after rejection; demonstrate an inclusive, team-building leadership style of problem solving and decision making; and are more likely to ignore rules and take risks.[22] So stereotypes can be counteracted with facts if aspiring leaders are armed with the knowledge of the contradictory evidence.

Wendy Shiba, executive vice president and general counsel of KB Homes, noted in a panel discussion on implicit bias, "When I was vetted for one of my jobs, the question that came back from the CEO was, 'Is she tough enough?' Think about what's behind that question. I really doubt if the male candidate was vetted the same way." She noted that even in the absence of questions motivated by bias, underlying stereotypes can, and do, affect access to promotions throughout the various hiring phases of a woman's career.

## CREATING A BALANCE

In order to close the gap and continue to develop women leaders in America and in the legal profession, we must recognize and contradict the erroneous stereotypes about women as leaders. However, the *Harvard Business Review* offered a cautionary note. The research found that, in an attempt to counteract stereotypes, women's leadership manuals, classes, and books can overreach ("Female Leaders Are Still Stereotyped," October 12, 2010): "Programs rely on bringing out the superwoman as a model of leadership. On the final day of our leadership program, a woman was invited to present her tips for getting ahead to a group of aspirational young female leaders. She was in her mid-forties, a professor and dean of a business faculty, and had just given birth to twins through IVF. She was immaculately put together, on stilettos all day. Can we do all that? Why do so many women's leadership programs send out this unrealistic and exhausting message?"[23]

While stereotypes exist that unconsciously serve as a bias against the promotion of women leaders, the notion that women can achieve everything all at once in every part of their life without a hair out of place can be just as damaging a stereotype to would-be leaders in our field. Do not believe that any of the women leaders you read about are perfect. They had days when kids spit up on their clothes or when they lost out on the promotion or when they forgot to bring the right presentation to the meeting. Leading is not about being perfect. Leading is about inspiring. Leading is about being honest about who you are and authentic to yourself. Leading authentically, blemishes and all, will engender a much greater following than pretending to be an unrelatable superwoman.

The reality is that myths and stereotypes exist. While no one can eliminate them, we can change the workplaces within our reach and take action to show that we are more than the sum of myths and stereotypes. More importantly, we can begin changing any stereotypes we have running on a negative loop in our own heads. As the authors of *Break Your Own Rules: How to Change the Patterns of Thinking That Block Women's Paths to Power* suggest, "We believe that for women to rise to the highest ranks in business, we need to unwind some of our traditional thinking and break our own rules. We have to rethink the conversations we are having in our heads and tell ourselves a new story. We all have thoughts and beliefs that limit our potential. Some of these beliefs come from our individual experiences; they take hold over the years. Others are a result of the gender stereotypes that are all around us. We get in our own way when we buy into limiting beliefs. But we don't have to continue repeating the same patterns. We have it within our power to change our own thinking and therefore change our future."[24] So how do we proceed? The rest of this book is designed to help you unlock the door to your leadership potential and guide you through a transformation in your leadership style on the path to success.

# 3

## What We Know

### What the Experts Tell Us about Women Leaders

*"How does one become a butterfly?" she asked pensively.*
*"You must want to fly so much that you are willing to give up being*
*a caterpillar."*

Trina Paulus, author

*We fought hard. We gave it our best. We did what was right and we*
*made a difference.*

Geraldine Ferraro, first female vice presidential candidate

*You cannot be afraid of who you are. Live your values. Live your life.*
*Just stand up, do what you need to do, and smile about it. Look them*
*in the eye and say, "If you don't like it, fire me, and I'll go find another*
*job, because I'm talented enough and I'm committed enough."*

Shelly Lazarus, chairman, Ogilvy & Mather

■ ■ ■

First of all, if you are on the fence about whether you have leadership potential, then let me clear it up for you: you do. It is work. Leading is hard, as you will see some of our interviewees lay out in great detail. But leading is rewarding. So often in the practice of law, especially in law firms, leadership is not emphasized. Law firms and government entities aren't set up like corporations, and many times lawyers leave the leadership lessons at the door. That is why this book pulls from an extensive library of research on leadership in other fields, specifically, those works focused on honing women's leadership skills, and tailors the lessons to the woman in the law. There's a great call to action in one of these books, written to equip women leaders with the tools of success:

> Visionary leadership and the ability to drive change do not come easily or naturally to most of us. But . . . leadership skills can be honed and improved. If you want to be viewed as senior leader material, you need to demonstrate that you can inspire others and make change happen. So step out of your comfort zone and rise to the challenge.[25]

That's what this book is meant to be—a challenge to you out there practicing law. The legal world is in desperate need of skilled and effective leaders. Leaders with a vision for the next chapter, or even the next book. Leaders with a focus on others as well as a focus on their own path. Leaders that know how to take charge and communicate and that didn't just fall into a leadership role because they were the de facto candidate.

So what *really* works? The "experts" use different lingo about what works for women leaders, but they all have similar central themes. The themes ring true. Before delving into some of the leading ideas and research out there, think about one of the most effective women leaders you have come across. You may know her personally, or she may be someone you have admired from afar. What skills did she possess that made her so effective? If you can't quite put your finger on it right now, think about her as you read through some of these themes and characteristics to see if you don't find similarities between what the experts say works and her set of qualities.

## WHAT LEADERSHIP LOOKS LIKE

Women leaders in law interviewed for this book had their own list of mentors and inspirational leader predecessors whose traits resonated with me and mirrored much of what the research bears out. To illustrate some of these tools and tips for leadership that surface in all leadership literature, let me describe two women whom I greatly admire. Both practiced law before moving into a new frontier. The first is a close friend and personal mentor who exhibits leadership on a local level. The second is a national figure whom I have never met but greatly admire.

The first woman has boundless optimism. She does not get upset publicly. She has undergone remarkable criticism at the hands of those who oppose her in certain situations and yet she is ceaselessly resilient. She always bounces back and maintains an optimistic attitude. She rarely criticizes her attacker, and when she does it is based in fact and in order to maintain her reputation for integrity. The second woman shares these skills.

The second woman holds unwaveringly to her values and sense of self. Regardless of whether those values are ridiculed, challenged, or criticized, she has held fast to who she is and what she believes. She never shies away from expressing her views and her positions, and everyone around her knows where she stands on the issues. The first woman does the same thing.

The first woman has had a clear vision of what she wanted for years. She developed a group of friends, supporters, and mentors that helped her know what had to be done to achieve that vision and to cheer her on as she worked toward the goal. She built a grassroots system of support so that when the time came to execute her dream, she had a strong network to help her achieve it and to celebrate her success once she attained it. There were setbacks and some conflicts along the way, but her forward-looking focus and incorporation of others into her vision allowed her to prevail. The second woman executed a very similar plan to attain her position.

The second woman blazed trails. She took risks that some would say were crazy. Bold, for sure. With her vision firmly in place in her mind's eye, she took steps that surprised many. She attained what most women could never imagine. She made friends and enemies along the way. She kept fully informed of the downside of the risks she was taking, and she took them anyway. While every risk didn't pay off, the risks she took deliberately ultimately led her down a path of unparalleled success and admiration. The first woman, while not taking risks with as broad a scope or as significant of a downside, took risks nonetheless and ultimately attained a prestigious goal because of her decision to buck the conventional wisdom.

Did you recognize any characteristics in those descriptions that mirror leaders you admire and seek to emulate? You will see similar stories in the accounts of judges and other leaders in law as well as in the research on what works for the most skilled women leaders in America today.

## THE BOOKS AND RESEARCH BEAR IT OUT

In *How Remarkable Women Lead: The Breakthrough Model for Work and Life,* one of the seminal leadership books on the market for women seeking to improve their leadership skills, the authors found five "clusters" of capabilities and tactics that resulted in successful women leaders.[26] The strategies this book highlights from the women the authors interviewed mirror many of the key principles discussed by the legal leaders interviewed for this book. The authors of *How Remarkable Women Lead*, however, spent years researching dynamic American women leaders and outlined five governing leadership principles. The first key for leaders the book highlighted is "Meaning." For lawyers, this simply means, what is it that motivates you? What makes you feel complete? What truly means something to you? Is it justice? equality? problem solving? Is it providing guidance? What made you become a lawyer? That's your "meaning." Whatever that core is for you will inspire you, guide your career, sustain your optimism, and generate positive emotions as you face the ups and downs of career and leadership twists and turns.

The authors label the next precept "Framing." This is exactly as you picture it. Being able to put a frame around something so that you can view situations clearly, avoid downward spirals, and move ahead to adapt and implement solutions. The next finding of their research centered on the concept of "Connecting." Well, this shouldn't come as a surprise in a book about women leaders. Women connect well, and they *need* to connect in order to succeed. Women particularly need to develop sponsors and followers as well as to collaborate with colleagues and supporters in order to establish themselves as successful leaders.

The fourth of the interconnected themes is "Engaging." This concept spans a much broader set of concepts than you might imagine. This is more than just being engaged in your life and setting out your course. If you want to develop into a successful, *engaged* leader, then the authors found that you must take ownership of opportunities as well as risks, you must have a voice that you use, and, maybe the hardest of all, you must face down your fears. The final strategy remarkable women leaders utilized is labeled "Energizing." Are you a runner? Do you do yoga? Are you a chef or a writer on the side? What is it that really gets you energized? The authors found that the most successful women can manage their energy reserves and even tap into that flow of energy to funnel it into leadership energy. A challenge for sure, but one that can be met.

There are many more books recounting "what works" if you are seeking to improve your leadership capabilities—far more than we could highlight in this little guide. However, a summary of some of the interesting works on leadership may be useful to you because of the way each frames leaderhip skills. You, like many practicing lawyers, may have preconceived notions of what it takes to lead and what you have to sacrifice if you choose to take it on. So while the themes track, in large part, from work to work, the approach differs. For example, in the book *How Women Lead: The 8 Essential Strategies Successful Women Know,* the authors outline eight concrete success strategies it takes for women to lead.[27]

The first strategy is to "Empower the Woman Leader Within." This means that you must learn to recognize, value, and practice the leadership strengths that you bring to your firm, association, company, or entity. Second, the authors urge you to "Own Your Own Destiny." Short of winning the lottery, there are concrete ways to define what success looks like for you that are grounded in your values, passions, and vision. They next recommend that you "Be the Architect of Your Career," meaning that you actually develop and acquire the credentials necessary to lead or succeed as you have defined it. "Advocate Unabashedly for Yourself" is the next recommendation, but it really just means that you have to become your own best advocate and develop the business case to position yourself for the next steps in your career. The authors also advise you to "Translate the Stories Numbers Tell to Drive Strategic Results," which, for legal purposes, means that you have to know the business and the numbers and the finance and not keep your head in the sand with regard to what keeps the company or firm moving forward.

No leadership book would be complete without talking about the followers, so here the authors say, "Create Exceptional Teams." This is more than just having good people around you on your team that support you—it is actually knowing how to grow teams into high-performing and functional assets that help you to achieve your goals. The next-to-last strategy is to "Nurture Your Greatest Asset—You." Modern America increasingly focuses on this priority of investing in yourself with care and time as well as integrating your personal life into your overall life. No one can function without personal relationships and inspirations to balance out the work pressures. Finally, the authors encourage all aspiring leaders to "Turn Possibilities into Reality." This skill set means more than just looking out for yourself and executing on your dream; it is also about making a difference in others' lives and helping other women on their way up.

Can you already see some themes emerging? Look at the individual example, the extensively researched *How Remarkable Women Lead*, and the practical *How Women Lead*. What themes do they have in common, and which ones do you see from your own experience in the practice of law? We see that these stories share the importance of teams and supporters, taking control of your career, and taking risks or seizing/creating opportunities.

Another savvy leadership book that builds on these concepts is *Break Your Own Rules*.[28] Here the authors present six "old school" rules—some of which might be found in the chapter on stereotypes—that they transform into six new rules that create leadership and success potential. The first old rule is "Focus on Others," which turns into the new rule "Take Center Stage." This moves you from the mind-set of always putting others first in your career to believing that you must take your own career dreams and aspirations seriously. Second, the old rule "Seek Approval" is transformed into the new rule "Proceed Until Apprehended." This old rule is a dominant concept in law firms, with its system of billing partners and partners managing client relationships. But this constant deferral becomes a mind-set, and in order to achieve success you have to change your thinking to proceed on your own authority and do so with confidence. The old rule "Be Modest" is replaced with the new rule "Project Personal Power." This doesn't mean you should be power hungry and thrive on vanity. Rather, the self-deprecation has to be set aside, and you must dial up your comfort level so as to feel at home in positions with power and authority.

Next, the authors replace the old rule "Work Harder" with the new rule "Be Politically Savvy," which is an incredibly applicable concept for legal practitioners whether in private practice, government, or a corporate law department. This concept means it's not just about the work—you have to instead build your career as if you were running for political office with a platform, sponsors, and a coalition. The old rule "Play It Safe" transforms into the new rule "Play to Win." This is a concept touted by many of the women legal leaders interviewed in this book who highlight the ability to take risks; these authors frame it by saying you should refuse to let others take the lead and learn to be comfortable living with risk. Finally, the authors say trash the old rule "It's All or Nothing" and replace it with the new rule "Both-And." Too many perfectionists have been derailed by breakdowns when they couldn't "have it all" or do it all, and so the authors caution that extreme thinking over having it all can push you off the path to success. Learn to do both—*I will train for the marathon and get that promotion by carving out time. I will be a good mother and a good lawyer by outlining a flexible work proposition for the managing partner.* Don't let the idea that you can't work twelve hours a day, six days a week deceive you into thinking you can't achieve the same modicum of success.

Can you hear that? It's MORE of the same. Couched in a different perspective and with a note about some of the negative myths that must go, but nonetheless repeating key precepts we see as necessary to transform you into an emerging leader. What are more of those recurring themes? Letting people around you know what contributions and successes you have delivered. Developing key relationships with mentors/sponsors and a team of supporters. Taking on more risk. Charting your own career and leadership course. We see this over and over again. *Play Like a Man, Win Like a Woman* suggests FOURTEEN basic rules for success (yikes!), but in looking at them (make a request, speak out, speak up, take a risk, don't anguish, follow the team leader, sit at the table, and laugh), we see the same behaviors that track from research to article to literature.

There are dozens more. All with wisdom. All with their own perspectives. But all with a similar message. Their titles include *How Great Women Lead; Women Lead the Way; Lean In: Women, Work, and the Will to Lead; The Next Generation of Women Leaders; Pearls, Politics, and Power; Womenomics: Write Your Own Rules for Success.* There are even more articles out there on women and leadership than there are books. They come equipped with top seven lists or top ten lists or the three key concepts to adopt. What this book will do is distill all this competing knowledge into big leadership themes.

## THE BIG LEADERSHIP THEMES

So let's boil it down. We'll tackle the key recurring themes here and then delve into how to apply them to your legal practice in chapter 4. One of the most frequent themes centers on power. Leaders take the power into their own hands. Leaders determine the course of their careers. Whether that means playing to win or owning your own destiny, the most effective leaders make affirmative decisions. They do not passively stand by and let their career happen without their direction. In order to lead, we see that you have to affirmatively make decisions. One of our interviewed judges urged, *Set your own timetable.* If you want something, then you cannot wait for it to happen to you because hard work and good fortune happen to coalesce. In *How Remarkable Women Lead*, the authors encourage, "There's nothing like feeling that you are in control to give you the courage to speak up, place yourself in the path of opportunities and take risks head-on. When you feel in control, your commitment and energy skyrocket. Better yet, you are less likely to be thrown by negative feedback or sidelined by attacks. Ownership is also the precursor to success, so don't wait to be chosen. Find ways to create new opportunities."[29] Deciding to chart your own course lays groundwork for several of the other recurring themes.

Two building block strategies for an effective leader to possess, albeit more intangible, are authenticity and optimism. Having a sense of yourself as well as a positive outlook are attributes featured in leadership research and interviews here. One judge describes how her background was so different from others when she first joined a private firm. She tried for a brief time to emulate those around her, but it just didn't work. She could not successfully work, win, or lead if she was copycatting what she saw from someone else. Over and over, leaders repeat the words "be true to yourself." It sounds a little like movie dialogue, but the truth is that there is a lot of copying going on in the world today, and there are far fewer authentic leaders with unique voices. The reason authenticity stands out is because it is becoming a rarity. The other recurring theme is optimism. Whether optimism comes naturally to you, or you work toward viewing life through a positive prism, it is imperative to have a positive outlook on your career, opportunities, and choices. Not only will that enable you to take bolder risks and make courageous decisions, but it will also equip you with the ability to bounce back from "failure" because you realize that a single setback does not dictate the end game. Additionally, people want to follow a leader with a positive outlook on the future and with the ability to frame issues in an encouraging and aspiring way. Nicholas Murray Butler once said, "Optimism is essential to achievement and it is also the foundation of courage and true progress."

If you are going to really effect change or make progress, then you will also have to adopt one of the most highlighted traits in the literature and from our interviewees: You Have to Take Risks. It is hard to know which risks are the right ones and which ones are foolish. It is challenging to navigate researching the merits of a risk without getting mired in indecision. How do you know how to step out into an uncomfortable place confident that it is the best direction to reach your true leadership potential? Start with small steps. In *How Remarkable Women Lead,* the authors clarify this risk-taking concept:

Just to set things straight, when we talk about risk, we're not talking about bet-the-company decisions. Nor are we suggesting that women leaders must throw the dice to determine where their careers should go next. We're talking about the risk and the fears inherent when you're challenged to leave your comfort zone behind. . . . Staying in your comfort zone will inevitably bore you over time. Step into the learning zone and resist your desire to head back to comfort, and you'll have expanded leadership capacity. . . . Deep down, you know that staying on course with the status quo is actually not safer than moving ahead. In terms of psychological well-being, "climbers" do better, despite the dangers of falling, than the people who stick to the safety of the low ground.[30]

But you can't take those risks without forethought and information. The way to guide your decisions is to apply the advice of experts to your vision. You cannot lead others without knowing what you are leading them toward. Leaders share a dream and direction that other people want to share and follow. The leadership vision goes beyond a written mission or vision statement. Your vision must be manifested in the actions, beliefs, values, and goals of your company or firm and in your people. The vision must be created by you and then lived out in the actions you take. Be warned, *Break Your Own Rules* shares, "Visionary leadership and the ability to drive change does not come easily or naturally to most of us. But . . . leadership skills can be honed and improved. If you want to be viewed as senior leader material, you need to demonstrate that you can inspire others and make change happen."[31]

Once you know what that vision is, then adopt the critical life and leadership skill of building relationships. This strategy touches every type of relationship you can encounter as a leader: those with mentors, sponsors, and supervisors; those with your followers and your team members; those with your colleagues, friends, and supporters. Each one of these types of relationships must be cultivated in order for you to develop as a leader. Leadership relationships are not manipulative strategies to advance your power. They start with genuine interest in and commitment to those you are developing the relationship with and, in reality, many of us have these relationships already in place—we just have not identified them as such.

Finally, communication plays an integral role in your leadership development. That can include "tooting your own horn," or acknowledging your contributions and successes to those that matter, speaking up and letting your voice be heard, and communicating your vision both up and down the career ladder. Ironically, women are frequently good communicators but refuse to communicate on their own behalf. How many of you will easily tout the skill and expertise of a friend, but yet refuse to do so for yourself? This shows how compatible these strategies are because hopefully you will have a friend through your relationships who will do the same for you.

You must be able to identify your contribution and achievements and skill-fully highlight them for supervisors or sponsors without seeming prideful or self-involved. You can communicate those messages in an authentic way that is met with a welcoming response if you cultivate your communication and inter-personal skills. Additionally, while it is admirable that you listen to all that is said in the room, you must also develop the skill set that enables you to interject when needed or speak up when you have a contribution. Unless you have a voice and exercise it, you will get passed over for leadership opportunities, and you will be unable to advance your vision.

So now that we have taken a look at what all the general business leadership books have to say about developing our leadership potential, let's explore these convenient sound bites and see if they really apply to those of us practicing law.

# 4

# How Does It All Work

## Applying What We Know to Women in Law

*A leader takes people where they want to go. A great leader takes people where they don't necessarily want to go, but ought to be.*
—Rosalynn Carter, former First Lady

*The leadership instinct you are born with is the backbone. You develop the funny bone and the wishbone that go with it.*
—Elaine Agather, chairwoman, JP Morgan Chase Dallas

*Our deepest fear is not that we are inadequate. Our deepest fear is that we are powerful beyond measure. It is our light, not our darkness, that frightens us. We ask ourselves, who am I to be brilliant, gorgeous, talented and fabulous? Actually, who are you not to be?*
—Marianne Williamson, author and lecturer

■ ■ ■

What does it look like? All this leading?

All too often we offer vague generalizations and platitudes about success and leadership, but it does not translate in real life. I don't know what area of law you practice, but in my practice I have seen laudable goals outlined in statutes and regulations fail the practical application test because the authors never worked in the industry or community they regulate. The goals and ideals of the policies or rule are commendable, but the plan laid out to execute the mission doesn't translate practically. Machines won't do what the regulators want them to do because the regulators have not tried to operate the machine, or work practices cannot be applied as written because the statute constructor never held the job. Words don't work unless they can be practically applied.

Do you ever feel like you are reading a book that is admirable but long on goals and lofty ideals and short on practical implementation? Like your real life couldn't possibly apply the theory?

That happens all the time. Especially with these personal growth and betterment books. For example, theoretically, risk taking leads to successful leaders. But you may feel your income is critical to your family's existence and, if you take a risk and fail, you could take your whole family down with you. Or if you are working in a company, an unwise risk could cause the company or division to fail. Besides, how can you know what risk to take?

"Investing in myself" means taking time away from everything to rejuvenate and regroup. That *is* an admirable ambition, but in what parallel universe will you find the time to do that? For those of us busy with a family and a job and board commitments, you get so overloaded "being" a leader that you have no time left for a great massage or to take up yoga. So how do you find the time so nothing else in your life suffers?

There are plenty of things you may feel you could do if you didn't have to wait for permission, but until you have the right role in the power structure, could doing that land you on the outs with the very powers necessary to leverage success? How do you know when running off in boldness to achieve great things is appropriate?

Not only are there practical concerns, some central voices on leadership offer conflicting advice. Be an active listener versus be the dissenter and speak assertively. Become a master at team building versus deferring to others. Which piece of advice should women follow? Does it depend on the circumstance, and if so, how do you gauge which advice applies when?

These next pages pick those nuggets of wisdom apart and translate them into practical application steps. Chapter 3 highlighted some of the biggest strategies that effective women utilize, and now we get to delve into them from the perspective of real working women in the law.

## THE LEADERSHIP LIST

Here are the characteristics this chapter looks at more in-depth and applies specifically to the practice of law:

- Be True to Yourself
- Be Optimistic
- Take Risks
- Chart Your Course
- Have a Vision (and Communicate It)
- Build Relationships (Including Mentors)
- Toot Your Own Horn
- Speak Up

But know that there are many more tools and "characteristics" that will help you cultivate your leadership potential: effectively delegating, developing productive mentoring relationships, treating yourself well, and more. The books and articles referenced in the appendix delve into these in more detail, but the ideas and strategies that follow include the ones that needed additional elaboration in the context of being a woman leading in law today.

## THE LEADERSHIP LANDMINES

In researching this book, I realized that there is more to this puzzle than just developing the skills that result in successful leadership. There are also behaviors to watch out for that could derail your leadership. You must consider this perspective on leadership as well as you hone your skills because knowing what could trip us up on the path to leadership is just as important as knowing the tools we need to climb the leadership ladder. In *True North: Discover Your Authentic Leadership*, the authors identify five types of destructive leaders that take actions that cripple their ability to lead and succeed.[32] The first set of bad actions is "impostors," who lack self-awareness and self-esteem. The next group is "rationalizers," who deviate from their values. Another characteristic that leads to defeat is found in "glory seekers," who are motivated by seeking the world's acclaim. Then come the "loners," who fail to build personal support structures. Finally are "shooting stars," who lack the grounding of an integrated life.[33]

Do you see the flip side to the coin of leadership skills we have studied? Authenticity is a critical skill, and if you fail to stay authentic and you lose your sense of values and guiding principles, then you become a rationalizer whom people refuse to follow. Developing relationships through mentors, sponsors, supporters, and followers is a much-touted leadership strategy, and failing to implement this strategy leaves you siloed and without support—a loner in the firm or organization who cannot achieve your goals. Understanding these weaknesses actually can help develop our strengths.

So now, having been forewarned, let's jump into our Leadership List!

## BE TRUE TO YOURSELF

*Be a first-rate version of yourself, not a second-rate version of someone else.*

— Judy Garland, singer and actress

*We don't accomplish anything in this world alone. Whatever happens is the result of the whole tapestry of one's life—all the weavings of individual threads from one to another that create something.*

— Sandra Day O'Connor, first female US Supreme Court justice

*Today you are You, that is truer than true. There is no one alive who is Youer than You.*

— Dr. Seuss

Authenticity. Not only do you hear about authentic leadership in all the books, it was a theme repeated over and over by the women judges and leaders we interviewed for the final chapters in this book. But this is the reality: Authenticity is both a critical element of becoming an effective and trusted leader, and yet it is one of the most overused concepts in America today. Isn't that an interesting conundrum? If you Google "authentic leadership" and even throw "women" in there to refine the search, you find almost a million and a half results. Yet you absolutely have to be who you are, and not emulate someone else, to have people put their faith in your leadership capabilities long-term.

In *True North,* the authors start with this concept about authenticity: "In large part the leadership vacuum has resulted from a misunderstanding of what constitutes an effective leader. During the past fifty years, leadership scholars have conducted more than one thousand characteristics, or personality traits of great leaders. None of these studies has produced a clear profile of the ideal leader. Thank goodness. If scholars had produced a cookie-cutter leadership style, people would forever be trying to emulate it. That alone would make them into personas, and others would see through them immediately. **The reality is that no one can be authentic by trying to be like someone else.** There is no doubt you can learn from their experiences, but there is no way you can be successful trying to be like them. People trust you when you are genuine and authentic, not an imitation."[34]

The book then goes on to identify what the research showed, after thousands of interviews, were the five most important dimensions of authentic leaders: pursuing purpose with passion, practicing solid values, leading with heart, establishing enduring relationships, and demonstrating self-discipline. The book identifies common themes that touch on many of our hallmark leadership characteristics:

> I described authentic leaders as genuine people who are true to themselves and to what they believe in. They engender trust and develop genuine connections to others. Because people trust them, they are able to motivate others to high levels of performance. Rather than letting the expectations of other people guide them, they are prepared to be their own person and go their own way. As they develop as authentic leaders, they are more concerned about serving others than they are about their own success and recognition.[35]

Being true to yourself. Internal harmony, clarity of purpose, and trust in your core beliefs. Integration of mind, body, and spirit. These are all pieces of authentic leadership. Authenticity continues to be praised as the single most important quality of leadership. Leaders must know, accept, and respect themselves.

If you picked up this book on a whim, not believing you could become a leader, or if someone gave you this book as a present and you randomly thumbed through it, landing on this page, then let me say this one thing to you: *You can lead.* While writing this book, I have learned that your life story defines your leadership.

That concept is repeated in books, articles, and the interviews we conducted. I read about the CEO of Starbucks, who grew up in the projects of Brooklyn watching his father's repeated career failures. He credits that background with giving him the motivation to create and lead a huge successful business. You'll hear about a judge who had to be labeled a secretary in order to get into an all-men's club with the other judges. I survived a traumatic family split at the age of twelve, worked just to have clothes for school, and learned how to drive for the first time when I started practicing law because I couldn't afford a car before then. No matter what your story, ease or hardship, poverty or affluence, extreme shyness or contagious outgoingness, it is the sum of your life events that enables you to lead uniquely as only you are capable. Each individual's story is the reason there is not one centralized list of what it takes to become a successful leader. While there are techniques that can assist you to develop, the foundation is built from your personal story and life experience. By applying some practical tips and tools and operating from a place of authenticity, you can lead in your life and in your career, and you can expand your sphere of influence.

*Lawyer Takeaway:* You may be naturally outgoing or shy. You may have come from a family of lawyers or be the first person in your family to go to college. You may have grown up without a shred of diversity in your life, or you may have every diverse quality that exists on this planet. Whatever your story is, **that is your story**. That is who you are. Regardless of what seems to be the "way to be" at your office, firm, or company, at the end of the day you must stay true to who you are and not try to fashion your leadership style or path to success by copying the path of someone you know or someone at your office. It will not ring true. This can be hard. Particularly if you are reading this and are still fairly new to the law. There is this innate chameleon instinct within people to blend into the surroundings they step into. Do not do that. You have achieved what you have because of who you are. You will not be happy pretending to be someone else. Plus, people will discover the inauthenticity, and they will not trust you, and in turn you won't be able to lead. Be you. If you're not sure who that is right now, then take some time to understand what that means. Establish your values and ideals and stay grounded in that sense of self regardless of the obstacles that may arise.

## BE OPTIMISTIC

*Definitely my sense of humor is a strength. When all else fails, I'll laugh. And optimism. I get up every day thinking today's going to be better than yesterday, and something wonderful is coming down the pipe.*

—Caryl Stern, president and CEO, UNICEF US Fund

*If you worry about everything that can go wrong, you would never do anything. You've got to be able to focus on the things that really matter and not lose too much sleep on the rest.*

—Julia Gillard, former prime minister of Australia

Closely connected to authenticity, and leading from your own personal story, is another pivotal leadership strategy: optimism. How you frame your story, your outlook on what comes your way, and the energy you exude can enable you to march into your leadership potential.

There are many benefits to possessing optimism: a general positive attitude not only motivates you but also motivates others who follow you and provides you with an ability to bounce back after a setback.

So what do leaders do, even those that are optimistic, when faced with setbacks? Start simply. Accept that failure from time to time is going to happen. In fact, failure is often the catalyst to more fully developing your leadership skill sets like coping, rebounding, learning from mistakes, and pressing on. Sometimes, things just don't work out as you may have envisioned. This is when you must separate the person, you, from the end result. This is where you can become more resilient. One way to approach this is to accept responsibility without blaming, evaluate what happened so you come away with having learned lessons, share the lessons with your team (and sometimes leadership), and apply them in the future. DO NOT continue to dwell on the past, however; move on with a revised set of goals.

Mike Baker, former CEO of ArthroCare, shares an honest and compelling assessment when discussing his failures: "I'm suspicious of somebody who's never failed, because you don't know how they're going to react when they do. Everyone is born to fail. Everyone is going to break down. What matters is not how often you have been on the canvas, but whether you get up, how you get up, and what you learn from it."[36]

In fact, *Forbes,* in its article entitled "Mandating Women at the Leadership Table: Why the Time is Now," notes the following as one of four skills women possess and why more female leadership is essential in the workforce: "**Resilience in applying lessons and learning from adversity**—Women leaders show a higher degree of resilience and assertiveness than their male counterparts. This coupled with their flexibility and interpersonal connection helps them shake off negativity and setbacks, learn what they need to from the experience, and use the setbacks to fuel their drive to succeed and overcome challenges."[37]

But even beyond setbacks, you must possess or learn to cultivate a baseline of optimism in order to effectively lead and encourage others. You can have a transformative effect on your team or followers by optimistically convincing others that they have the ability to achieve levels of performance beyond those they thought possible. Leaders can paint an optimistic and attainable view of the future for their followers. You, with a well-communicated, optimistic vision, can move others from being stuck with "how things are done around here" to "how things could be done better." In their own lives, strong leaders rise above petty thoughts and steer clear of self-defeating inner dialogue. Leaders that have control of these strategies and skills are more likely to remain cool and in control in a crisis, and are less likely to let negative influences bring them down and find themselves spinning in those self-defeating cycles that can cripple even the best of leaders.

*How Remarkable Women Lead* emphasizes how important it is to **practice** optimism. Psychologists believe that you can learn optimism, particularly if you learn where pessimism comes from so that you can stop the downward spiral. There are two tactics recommended to improve your own optimism: *disputation,* which involves re-examining the situation and consciously separating how you experienced the incident emotionally from what really happened, and *finding alternatives,* which means looking for other explanations as to why events unfolded as they did.[38] The authors point out, "Every woman leader we met was an optimist, and it really doesn't matter who was born one and who developed the skill. With a little bit of practice, it will be your skill, too, and not just one to deploy at work."[39] While a positive disposition can be largely hereditary, you can gravitate toward the top of your own bandwidth of natural tendency. More importantly, if you can find things that you liked as a child, things that make you passionate, or recent activities that gave you tremendous fulfillment, then you can begin filling your life with things that are more inclined to provide you with an optimistic and energetic disposition. Once you have spent time reflecting on these pieces, you can intentionally choose activities that will cause you to have a greater sense of optimism than you would if you filled your time with more meaningless endeavors.

*Lawyer Takeaway:* Whether you are naturally an Eeyore or a Tigger, you can train yourself to positively frame your life messages. *Optimism* does not translate to *delusional* for those of you natural pessimists who are looking at this section apprehensively. Nor does it mean idealism, as some skeptics suggest (though a measure of idealism may help you lead). It means you do not allow failures and setbacks to derail your trajectory. After allowing yourself to feel the sting of not reaching the achievement you had set your sights on, move on. Find out what lessons you learned from the experience and start searching for the next opportunity. That may mean your path has changed. Embrace it.

Optimism also means you get back to doing things that bring you joy. If you haven't felt joyful about much lately, then think back to previous years and times when you were happy or fulfilled. See how to incorporate those things that brought you joy into your life today. Finding outside activities to increase your optimism level is often necessary for lawyers. All too often lawyers are fighting, prosecuting, or defending criminals, or buried under thousands of documents to review—essentially embroiled in negativity, which can really mess with your outlook and ability to take positive steps to lead and succeed. But true joy and fulfillment are attainable, and they are also contagious and will allow you to build a base or team from which you can lead. Take time out this next week and listen to yourself interact with colleagues, with friends, with clients, or with supervisors. How do you frame things? Do you see the negativity from a case or a challenging work relationship seeping into all aspects of your thinking and speaking? Can you begin by taking simple steps to reframe the negative voice you hear internally with factual and unemotional responses? Once you are working on what you hear internally, or what you are exposed to externally by counteracting it, how you interact and engage externally with prospective mentors, sponsors, and followers will begin sounding more optimistic, too.

## TAKE RISKS

*I've not ceased being fearful. I've gone ahead despite the pounding in my heart that says: turn back, turn back, you'll die if you go too far.*
— Erica Jong, author

*We stand in a circle whose circumference is bounded by the circle of our own fears.*
— Gandhi

*You gain strength, courage, and confidence by every experience in which you really stop to look fear in the face. You must do the thing which you think you cannot do.*
— Eleanor Roosevelt, former First Lady

Willingness to take risks. This is one of the most oft-cited characteristics of a great leader. But what does it really mean? How do you differentiate good risks from just making a stupid move? And when is the right time to take a risk—anytime? The reason "taking risks" appears as a recurring leadership theme is because risks are necessary to make changes happen—that can be personal risk, risk to followers, and risk to the organization or group you lead. So understanding and knowing how to hone your "risk-taking" skill set is critical if you want to lead successfully.

First of all, risk taking requires a certain frame of mind. Certain of us are intrinsically designed to feel comfortable taking risks. Those risk takers could be just as comfortable bungee jumping as starting their own solo practice. To take risks, you have to be willing to step outside your comfort zone. Why do many of us cling to a comfort zone, even if it is not fulfilling us? Some women with leadership potential fear the unknown or uncertainty, which can hold them back. *The devil you know is better than the devil you don't know.* In *How Remarkable Women Lead*, the authors wisely counsel, "Learning to face your fears is actually the best part of accepting opportunity. When you do, you'll find they are far less powerful than they seemed. You'll also experience the lightness of being that comes with getting back in control."[40] Don't you love that turn of phrase? It's not "risk taking"—it's **accepting opportunity!** Sheryl Sandberg, chief operating officer of Facebook, spoke about the opportunity that presented itself with Google (her former position before her employment at Facebook) in her book *Lean In: Women, Work, and the Will to Lead:* "I was supposed to be the first business unit general manager. But there were no business units. There was nothing to generally manage. And he [Eric Schmidt, CEO of Google] kind of put his hand on my paper and he was like, 'If you're offered a seat on a rocket ship, you don't ask what seat. Get on the rocket ship.' And I did." Sandberg had come from a land of stability—Harvard, chief of staff to Treasury Secretary Lawrence Summers—and yet she had to be reminded that sometimes the risk seems scary but is too great an opportunity to pass up.[41]

The other mind-set required to step out into the unknown is confidence. You not only have to be confident in yourself and your capability, but you have to be able to demonstrate confidence to those followers and colleagues around you in order to lead them to uncertainty. You may know that the risk is a smart one, but unless you can successfully exhibit that to those around you, then no one will support you in taking the risk.

You also have to be willing to take on a challenge. Risk is not easy or everyone would do it. Risk-taking ability would not be a distinguishing characteristic of great leaders if it meant a simple path that anyone could follow. Smart risks come with rewards, but to make it to the other side you have to be willing to tackle tough challenges and obstacles.

Confidence cannot be overemphasized as a skill that must be possessed or developed as you become a risk taker. All too often, leading women will be interviewed—from the head of the International Monetary Fund to a presidential cabinet official to a CEO of a Fortune 500 company—and they use language suggesting that they feel like a fraud or are scared to raise their hand in a group of impressive peers. These are the women who have made it. You would think that as lawyers, we would have confidence in spades. Wrong. Repeatedly we see lack of confidence as the Achilles' heel in women achieving the next promotion, managing the significant case, landing the new client, or even applying for the right job. You will never be able to take smart risks until you are confident in your own ability to make smart choices.

Shona Brown, the senior vice president of Google, highlights this confidence-risk partnership: "I don't think that I'm a thrill-seeker. I'll use skiing as the analogy because I like to jump off cliffs. But I generally jump off cliffs that I'm relatively confident I'm going to land and that if I don't, it's not dangerous. There are people who like to jump off cliffs who think their skill is better than it really is. They hurt themselves. There are people who are quite skilled but are afraid to jump. I like to be at that point where you're about to jump and your stomach is going, woo!"[42]

That is a perfect analogy of the kinds of risks you should take. You have researched and studied and investigated and you feel relatively confident that you are going to land on your feet. And if you don't land on your feet, you will not bring everyone down around you. This is not to say you get mired in the research mode, which freezes your decision-making capability. There is always more information available, and it is easy to get stuck in information paralysis where you do nothing and just continually analyze the possibilities. However, it also does not mean you won't sometimes take big risks. Here's another great perspective on how to approach risk:

> Just to set things straight, when we talk about risk, we're not talking about bet-the-company decisions. Nor are we suggesting that women leaders must throw the dice to determine where their careers should go next. We're taking about the risk and the fears inherent when you're challenged to leave your comfort zone behind. . . . In other words, everything is familiar and that gives you comfort. Take one step beyond, and you begin to feel uncomfortable. For the most part, women exercise more caution than men. . . . It's still true that reward is proportional to risk—nothing ventured, nothing gained. If success isn't enough to motivate you, consider personal growth. Basic human learning theory says that you grow by exposing yourself to new challenges. That doesn't happen without a willingness to step into your "learning zone." What happens when you cross into this new territory? It's scary! It's the place where your fears reside—perhaps fear of failure, of being judged, of losing control, of getting hurt. It's the place where you'll make more mistakes. But it's also exhilarating! It's the place where you develop, you experience the thrill of newness. You're alert. Staying in your comfort zone will inevitably bore you over time. Step into the learning zone and resist your desire to head back to comfort, and you'll have expanded leadership capacity.[43]

So let's talk about what kind of risks to take. Having identified that some of us are more risk-averse than others, you have to start by building your risk muscles. We all know that the more we exercise, the stronger we get. And the stronger we get, the more comfortable we become exercising. As you build your risk muscles, you'll find yourself getting into a cycle in which your sense of self-confidence and power will be continually expanding. Several studies note that women in certain situations tend to have a lower risk threshold because of extenuating circumstances like having young children and/or being the primary breadwinner in the family. Understandably, those circumstances can make you wary of change that could impact those around you that rely upon you. However, you must still begin to take on risk selectively. The benefit of taking on smaller risks before taking on large-scale risks is that it not only builds your risk muscles, but it also begins to develop your reputation as someone capable of taking "smart" risks. It also equips you with the skills necessary to analyze risky situations so that you can distinguish a smart risk from a bad risk. Note, these risks don't have to be all career risks. Take a language course. Plan an event. Sign up to be on the board of a charity you love. Take a practical step that requires you to step out a little. Sometimes practicing outside of work allows you the freedom to feel more comfortable if the risk doesn't pay off. Then you can move to smaller risks in your career. As you grow and develop, you build a reputation at work for being a smart risk taker and you build a new "comfort zone" where you become comfortable analyzing and taking risks.

One way to approach your first few risks is to ban "paralysis by analysis" because you want to cover all ten things that could go wrong. This kind of thinking restricts creativity and innovation. If you have a natural inhibition to risks, work to overcome it. Think positive, see a plan, and change your perspective to focus on the benefits.

The authors of *How Remarkable Women Lead* interviewed women leaders and asked them how they identified an opportunity. The women interviewed didn't have greater luck than the average woman; they had prepared minds where they could assess risk and opportunity. The recommendation that came out of those interviews was, "Start with the upside. Most of us approach risk assessment by listing what can possibly go wrong. We're pros at filling out that list. Flip this around. First imagine the very best that could happen. Write it down and make it tangible—what you will learn, what skills you will build, what options you will have, what new people you will meet. Then talk to five people who know something about that opportunity, and ask them to imagine the best that could come out of it."[44] They go on to say that if you don't know experts, then imagine how someone you admire would approach the opportunity. Look at leaders and innovators like Steve Jobs and write down what ideas you get by examining the risk/opportunity from a different perspective. Even write down your fears. Name them so you can confront them. Writing down the upside as well as the ideas that are holding you back, like failure or embarrassment, helps you take the leadership role in your own life to make a credible and valuable decision. Once you have dismissed the illogical fears, you can more credibly approach the downside and understand if it's an appropriate risk to take.

Another step to moving you toward a more risk/opportunity-taking mind-set is to acknowledge the risks you have already taken. For example, I tend to be risk-averse because of a number of past circumstances that cultivated that fear of the unknown or of failure. However, when I look at decisions I have made on my own, without the influence of parents or a spouse or a boss, I see that I have taken calculated risks like moving cities and changing jobs. That enables me to frame risks in terms of something I know and have done and can do again. Every time we embrace taking a chance and trying something new, we're stepping up to the plate as leaders. You have taken a risk if you've done any of the following:

- Applied for a new position or taken on an assignment that's a stretch from what you currently do;
- Moved to a new company;
- Spoken up in a meeting, especially with an opinion that may not be popular;
- Advocated for someone on your team;
- Asked for a raise;
- Ended a client contract because it wasn't serving the client or your organization;
- Taken an international assignment or relocated; or
- Chaired a visible committee in your company or within a professional organization.

I bet if I was sitting down with you over a cup of coffee, you could identify more than one of those items on the list as decisions you have made. See, you ARE a risk taker. Frame your next decisions and opportunities that feel too risky in terms of decisions you have executed successfully in the past.

Reframe risk taking to give you this positive perspective: "Making a courageous move is also the highest form of service," said James Strock, author of *Serve to Lead*. "Courage, always, when you strip it down, is about love for someone or something. And that's what leads people to do extraordinary things and to put themselves at risk."[45] What if, in taking the risk and seizing the opportunity, we realized we were doing it for the greater good? That the risk is ultimately designed to benefit our followers, our company, our firm, our clients, or our colleagues? That courageous decision makes us successful and sought-after leaders.

*Lawyer Takeaway:* I know sometimes it can feel like you have the weight of the world on your shoulders. You may be single or married. A mother, daughter, sister, wife, friend, colleague, client, advisor, and on and on. Sometimes taking a risk feels like a too-foolish gamble. On the other hand, you may be such a risk taker that you move foolishly into a decision without doing the necessary groundwork. So start small. Analyze your risk threshold. Take a risk-threshold test. If you find out that you are, like many women, risk averse, then make small steps toward stepping out in risk. Leaders have to be willing to effectuate change, so you must make something change. If you are underpaid, ask for a raise and present reasons why you earned it. If you want to run for office, begin a grassroots effort by running for director of your neighborhood association or school board or bar section. If you need to find a new job in order to have leadership opportunity, ask for new opportunities where you are currently located. Go negotiate the price of a suit at Macy's. Get past the feeling of doom if someone says "No!" We are lawyers. We calculate risks on cases all the time. Is it a winner? Will I get paid? Is there credible evidence? Apply these legal skills to your own personal risk development. Do the groundwork. Know what you're asking for and what you want. Enlist supporters and marshal the evidence. Then take a step. Any step. But take one calculated small risk. It will build. As will your risk-taking muscles.

## CHART YOUR COURSE

> *True success is how you define it for yourself. All too often, women's definition of success is based on what they believe others expect of them. Free yourself up to define success based on your own values, passions, and vision.*
>
> —Jill Flynn, *Break Your Own Rules*

> *Your work is to discover your work, and then, with all your heart, to give yourself to it.*
>
> —Buddha

**W**hat do you want to do when you grow up? Do you remember getting asked that question from the age of three to twenty-three? If you're anything like I was, then the answer probably changed dramatically over those interim decades. Well, leaders know where they are headed, and all the experts agree that leaders take their destiny into their own hands. In *How Women Lead: The 8 Essential Strategies Successful Women Know,* the authors use two of their eight total success strategies to focus on this single issue; the first strategy is "Own Your Own Destiny" and the very next one is "Be the Architect of Your Career."[46] In that second strategy, recent research shows that "women who achieve most are also women who define success in their own terms and integrate achieving high financial goals with creating a business that reflects their passions.... Women should think of their businesses as million-dollar businesses from Day One. This drives how they structure the business, the decisions they make, and the way they present themselves and the business."[47] This entire premise highlights that all too often women impose self-limiting views on their own dreams—believing that their dreams are unrealistic or that certain levels are unreachable. While encouraging women to break free of the boundaries that stifle their ambition, the authors simultaneously remind potential leaders that building a career requires each woman to take responsibility for achieving her own goals: "Building a career takes a little serendipity; a bit of being in the right place at the right time; a considerable amount of flexibility, courage, and belief in yourself; and a lot of risk taking and hard work. Most important of all, it involves taking responsibility for propelling yourself to achieve your goals."[48] This does not mean the path is linear, and in fact there is no way you can plan your career from day one and never deviate. In fact, many authorities on the topic describe successful women's careers more like waves in an ocean than an ascending ladder. Life intervenes. Women have children and aging parents and health scares. Plus, careers are far too unpredictable and flexible, and there are circumstances beyond your control. However, the constant is that you have a responsibility to ensure that you re-chart and recalibrate as needed so you can fulfill the leadership potential you have.

In *Break Your Own Rules,* the authors encourage you to break certain rules that often center on you being told what to do versus moving forward under your own initiative: "The Old Rules say that being liked is more important than being promoted, that ambition is selfish, that we must ask for permission before acting, and that we fear hearing the word 'no.' These are the rules to break."[49]Another obstacle facing many would-be leaders, the authors highlight, is a sense of obligation to seek approval rather than to proceed on their own authority and do so effectively and with confidence.

The authors use a great illustration of a young female lawyer in DC to drive home their point that certain situations require you to make the decision first instead of waiting for permission to be granted:

> Early one morning, both Sarah and her colleague Rich received an email from one of the senior partners at the firm, asking for assistance. *Do either of you have expertise in the arena of eminent domain?* The partner was working on a complicated case with one of the firm's largest clients, and he needed someone to help him prepare his brief. Sarah was excited: she had recently written a research memo on this very topic. She acted fast. She sent an email to her manager, asking for permission to assist the senior partner with the assignment. She got the nod within minutes and was good to go. As she replied to the initial email, explaining that she had just written a research memo on eminent domain and would be thrilled to take the assignment, Rich and the senior partner walked by her office. They were elbow-to-elbow and deep in conversation. Rich already had the job. He had not stopped to ask anyone's permission; he had walked right into the senior partner's office and expressed interest. Rich spent the next month working closely with the firm's senior partner, helping their prized longtime client. He was building a name for himself. It takes courage to act before getting the green light from your boss, but sometimes you just have to do it. Sarah felt the sting of the missed opportunity, but she managed to learn a difficult lesson about acting decisively and stepping up independently to take the initiative.[50]

Researchers, experts, and authors all agree that taking charge of your career is a way of creating your own luck. Listen to this advice from authors who talked to thousands of the most remarkable women leading today:

> People who take responsibility feel they can shape their destiny. They feel in control, and that gives them the confidence and commitment to pursue their passions, even when the odds of winning are not great. Also,

when things go badly or the feedback is negative, it won't knock you down, because you know you have the power to create a better outcome tomorrow . . . Ownership is what psychologists call having an internal locus of control in your life. That means you believe your destiny is up to you. The opposite is an external locus of control, believing that things happen to you regardless of your effort and behavior; events shape your life, not you. In general, people with an internal locus can be more confident and self-motivated, less afraid to take risks.[51]

There are numerous tricks and techniques to transform that internal focus to an external one if you are prone to the former: Get input from work associates to assess what aspects of your professional situation are in your control and ask how other people perceive their ability to shape the outcome in the same situations. The focus must be moving from waiting for other people to decide your path to determining where you want to go and taking steps to get yourself there.

*Lawyer Takeaway:* Do you know what you want? That might be step one. (Read on if you want to find out more about vision.) But if you do know what you want, then sit down and find out where you can start taking affirmative steps to make that a reality. If your end goal is to become an executive director of a nonprofit, then begin by learning areas of nonprofit law and sitting on boards or chairing committees for nonprofit and charitable organizations that have a well-respected history. If you want to one day serve on corporate boards, then seek out mentors who have done so or individuals in key companies that know what is the most sought-after skill set. Maybe it means transitioning from your current job or obtaining an MBA to partner business with your legal acumen. If you want to become the go-to solo practitioner in estate law in your community, then begin by volunteering in elder centers and legal aid clinics where you can hone your skill set through pro bono opportunities. Whatever your goal, write it down, find advisors to bounce ideas off, and then write out the next three steps you plan to take to move you closer to that outcome.

## HAVE A VISION (AND COMMUNICATE IT)

*I define leadership as having three parts: first is seeing what needs to be done to make things better or seeing a problem that needs fixing; second is having the vision, the skill, and the wherewithal to change*

*the system; and third is the most important task of mobilizing the energy of others to organize and act in ways to achieve that vision.*
—Susan J. Herman, president, ACLU

*Walt Disney told his crew to "build the castle first" when constructing Disney World, knowing that vision would continue to serve as motivation throughout the project. Oftentimes when people fail to achieve what they want in life, it's because their vision isn't strong enough.*
—Gail Blanke, president and CEO, Lifedesigns

*If you have a sense of purpose and a sense of direction, I believe people will follow you. Democracy isn't just about deducing what the people want. Democracy is leading the people as well.*
—Margaret Thatcher, former prime minister of Great Britain

This section could be split into two topics because vision and communication are each integral strategies in implementing an effective leadership path. But because so much of what leaders are responsible for communicating is vision, it makes sense to tackle them together.

Successful women leaders have vision. They have both a personal vision and a career vision, whether it is for their personal promotion or for their firm or their company or their office section. To implement your vision, set goals aligned with your values and work toward those goals consistently, use your values to guide your decisions and to keep you on track, and ensure your vision is clearly articulated and shared with others so everyone can be a part of creating and achieving the goals.

But *vision* sounds so intangible. It is hard to provide practical steps to ideas that you carry in your head. Plus, vision can be personal and professional. It can be your driving goals, but it can also be your sense of purpose. In *How Remarkable Women Lead*, an outstanding leader was interviewed about her success, and she kept bringing the conversation back to her purpose: "When you have a higher purpose in mind and it's shared by the team, leading is easier. You are not tripped up by the little stuff—who is ahead of you, or what department is outperforming yours, or a million other distractions. With purpose, setting goals becomes easier. You find the courage to face new challenges."[52] The authors of

*How Women Lead* assert that you cannot be a successful leader without discovering and owning your own guiding vision.[53] Repeatedly they highlight that your vision has to be a holistic understanding of your life and your career and that you don't have to adopt a traditional timeline for your leadership metrics or assume that your career progression will follow a straight track. The reality is, detours occur. And as much of the research shows, that detour can become your passion, your opportunity, or your new path.

In addition to those intangible and aspirational aspects of vision, it has some concrete execution forms as well. In that crossover between vision and communication, we see that great bosses, influential presidents, persuasive lawyers, and even strong teachers know how to effectively motivate people to get on board with their vision through words and gestures. They use both verbal and nonverbal skills to convey powerful emotion. Many women have skills that intrinsically work well with developing a guiding vision and motivating people to follow that vision. Women can be better at motivating others because they often show appreciation for the efforts of others, express their thoughts and feelings, and display enthusiasm.

To have an effective vision to lead, make sure you set direction and purpose (whether it's for your office, or a committee on which you serve, or a project that you manage); inspire loyalty by involving your team; show the unique strengths and values of your team; inspire enthusiasm and commitment in your team or staff; help your team, supporters, or followers believe they are part of something bigger than just the day-to-day work; regularly communicate and share with your work group; and challenge people to stretch and outdo themselves.[54]

Effective women leaders also have good communication skills, which, as you can see, are critical to execution of a vision. They are excellent listeners. They hear what other people are saying to them and they respond appropriately. They tell people what they need to know in clear and compelling words. Their communications are frequent and to the point. Can you see how this might present a challenge for lawyers who often use extra words as bonus points? For strong communicators and leaders, people know where they stand and what is expected of them.

Communication is a two-way street. You must be an effective communicator. But you must also be able to understand what people are trying to communicate to you, sometimes with less-than-ideal clarity. If you cannot hear and distill the feedback from your team, your supervisors, your support staff, your mentors, and your colleagues, then you will be unable to communicate with them. People who are not heard are less likely to hear your message in return.

When you are the one communicating, the avenues in which you must become an effective communicator can be overwhelming. You will have to communicate within your firm or company in an organizational capacity; you will have to provide (and receive) feedback; you will have to communicate with your smaller teams; you will have to persuade (which we learned from law school moot court), and that can include public speaking as a communication medium; and then you will even have to manage the communication messages running through your head. And each of those mediums has its own subset of communication pitfalls and prizes. Take, for example, communicating within an organization (your own practice, your nonprofit, your government agency, your law firm) where you are providing information and, hopefully, consistent messaging. You have to communicate upward, downward, and laterally, all while managing any gossip or negativity. That communication is not just oral in this era of e-mail as the way law firms and companies do business. People forget that the inflection and moderation you can execute through oral communication is lost in writing. So an effective leader learns how to manage all these different forms of communication within the firm or company. You also have to provide feedback to those who are part of your team. This presents constant challenges for leaders today because the leader and/or the recipient may not want to provide or hear anything that is less than positive. But in order to keep a team headed toward the goal, feedback must be provided regardless of its positive or negative implications. As an emerging leader, you must weigh objective and subjective and select the right time and environment in which to communicate.[55]

Additionally, a leader wants the most effective and productive team helping her achieve her goal. Brenda Barnes, former CEO of Sara Lee Corporation, encourages truly valuing your team charged with following the vision: "How do you unleash fifty thousand people to get the job done? It goes back to how do you let them help. We changed from, 'Let me tell you the answer' to 'What do you think we ought to do?' Did we make them feel like they were worthwhile, or did we make them feel like they weren't at all?"[56] In order to implement a vision, you have to have participation and buy-in from your entire team and set of supporters. That concept partners well with delegating, which is another communication and action activity that strong leaders develop:

Weak leaders tend to micro-manage; that's when you assign a task to some-one else but then, instead of trusting them to get the job done, focus all of your energy nitpicking and criticizing. A good leader puts her trusted team members to work so she can free up her time to make long-range plans for the future. The strong female in charge knows how important it is to have key people in her corner who are well suited to the jobs that she needs them to complete. This keeps her at the helm of the plan, focused on long-range goals and ensuring that the group can continue to maximize productivity, stay motivated for the future and attain everything they set out to![57]

*Lawyer Takeaway:* What do you want? Today, next year, ten years from now, at the end of your career? You have to figure that out first. Then develop some concrete steps you can take to move you closer to that vision. Start small. You don't have to set your life career vision today. Maybe you just set your vision for your family at the end of the year. Identify a specific area of your life and a spe-cific period of time. But then start thinking bigger. Now that you are seeing how to reframe the voice in your head and take risks, you should be able to develop a vision for yourself that reflects the best and most successful you could be. What is it you really want to achieve? Who is it you really want to lead? And where do you want to lead them? And take note, this can change over time. What your vision may have been five years into the practice of law may be radically differ-ent than what your vision is after fifteen years of practicing. If you don't take the time every year to look at your changed circumstances and readjust your motivating vision, you may find yourself adrift ten years into your career. Cir-cumstances change and they take the vision on the journey with them.

Then start working on your communication skills. First, do you actively lis-ten when others are speaking? Stop yourself over the next week in the hallways and in team meetings and find out if you hear what people say or if you are just thinking about the next response to the issue being discussed. Then, work on your communication skills. What words motivate people? If you struggle with communicating, take a class at a local junior college. Start practicing with your spouse or your friends to see if your vision translates into an understandable form when you begin to speak about it. Identify where you may have commu-nication weaknesses at your office—up or down the pipeline—and then think of ways you can improve your communication. Speaking more positively and effectively can change your trajectory internally. Make sure you fix the communication problems in front of you before you move into a new challenge or frontier.

Make sure you have a vision that is guiding you first. It is that vision that will help you see whether your response should be yes or no, now or never, or stay or move.

## BUILD RELATIONSHIPS (INCLUDING MENTORS)

*One of the most important ways to be successful is actually to create an army of people who are rooting for you. It's nice to have the support of the person you work for, or a board, but the most important support you can get is from the troops.*

—Anne Mulcahy, CEO, Xerox

*Leadership should be born out of the understanding of the needs of those who would be affected by it.*

—Marian Anderson, singer, UN delegate, civil rights activist

*You have to look at leadership through the eyes of the followers and you have to live the message. What I have learned is that people become motivated when you guide them to the source of their own power and when you make heroes out of employees who personify what you want to see in the organization.*

—Anita Roddick, businesswoman and human rights activist

There are numerous relationships this theme can encompass. Your relationships with those you lead, your team, and your followers. Your relationships with your bosses and supervisors. Your relationships with those who mentor you, support you, connect you, sponsor you, and encourage you. Your relationships with colleagues and your network. There are so many different facets of relationship building, and all are critical to leading successfully.

The benefit of establishing enduring relationships is mutual for you, as a leader, and your counterpart in the relationship. Many people demand personal relationships with their leaders before committing themselves fully to their job or service or following or promotion. In *True North*, the authors indicate that people "insist on access to their leaders, knowing that trust and commitment are built on the openness and depth of relationship with their leaders. In return, people will demonstrate great commitment to their work and loyalty to the company."[58] Libby Sartain, former senior vice president of Yahoo, says, "I believe you serve those you lead by giving them the tools, knowledge, and mentorship they need to get their jobs done. Forming good relationships above you, on the same level with you, and below you is how people succeed in the workplace. This is accomplished by thinking about what others need, not what you need."[59]

Successful women leaders are great at relationship building. They work at it. Maintaining and building strong relationships is an integral part of what they do on a daily and weekly basis. They understand an organization runs on relationships and that strong relationships build commitment. A woman's skill at relationships is one of the intrinsic qualities that equip her well for leadership.

One of the types of relationships that many of the women I spoke with highlighted were their mentor/sponsor relationships that helped them get to where they are and succeed once they did. ABA President Laurel G. Bellows (2012–2013) recently highlighted the significance of mentor and sponsor relationships:

> A mentor alone is not enough to catapult a talented woman lawyer up the career ladder. For real career advancement, women need sponsors as well as mentors. What's the difference? A mentor gives advice, serves as a sounding board and makes suggestions, for example, on strengthening your work or searching for a job. A sponsor is an active campaigner (inside and outside an organization) on behalf of a particular woman. Even when a sponsor's protégé isn't present, a sponsor will tout her abilities: "Why not consider Rebecca for this position/for this client's team/to handle a particular case? She'll be terrific."

> One Catalyst survey found that women who have mentors are less likely to be promoted than women with sponsors. Another Catalyst study found that, while mentoring is essential for leadership development, it is insufficient for advancing to top levels. A sponsor "can propel a protégé to the top of a list or pile of candidates or even eliminate the list itself." To find a sponsor, identify influential senior-level people in your company, in your local bar association or industry networking groups, or in the American Bar Association. Then sell your potential sponsor on your performance

and potential. That means vocalizing your strengths with conviction and fully endorsing yourself.[60]

The significance of mentor and sponsor relationships nearly merits its own section, and that is why much of this relationship-building segment is focused on those. Every article, research paper, and book I read highlighted the value both of these types of relationships create:

- "According to Cathy Bessant of Bank of America, 'Without sponsorship, you don't get opportunities. To take center stage, you have to have opportunities. Only sponsorship early on delivers that.' We take sponsorship advice a step further and advocate that women put together their own 'board of directors,' a group of five or six sponsors. This team of advocates offers you active and strategic support to help you proceed to the next level."[61]
- "Mentors draw on their experiences and wisdom to guide you with sage counsel. It's good to have mentors, and the more the merrier. But mentors don't change the trajectory of your career. A sponsor makes things happen. He or she works on your behalf, getting involved with your career. A sponsor also protects you when the chips are down or when you've made a mistake. Sponsors do good in many not-so-obvious ways. For example, your sponsor can help you when you're not in the room, by battling gender biases that unfortunately still persist. . . . Because they've gone before you, sponsors can be expert guides around the booby traps and dead ends that exist in any organization. . . . Finally, a sponsor can be your best source of feedback and can help you maintain your emotional well-being when you face development issues."[62]
- "A mentor is someone you can go to for advice about a challenging project you have undertaken, how to get over a hurdle, or how to deal with specific issues. Mentors serve as sounding boards, let you know if you are on the right track, and help you think through a situation. Mentors do not give you the solution; they help you think about the range of solutions. 'I can't say enough about having the right mentors,' says Debra Hanna. 'Having someone other than your boss who knows your strengths to bounce ideas off when you are making stressful decisions and choices, someone who will challenge your thinking, and help you make solid decisions is incredibly valuable.'"[63]

As you can see, one of the most critical aspects of developing your leadership potential and identifying the pathways for opportunity is to find and build relationships with women who can serve as mentors and sponsors. But don't forget, for those of you who are succeeding and developing, you must in turn serve as a mentor and sponsor to those coming along behind you. As one author encouraged, "Share the experience, knowledge, and insights you have gained along the way—the things you know now that you wish someone had told you earlier. . . . The experience of expanding others' horizons expands your own horizons as well, so in giving back, you also enrich yourself. Begin reaching back as early as possible."[64]

The other side of creating and building relationships is that of a successful or emerging leader in a position to make hiring decisions. Exceptional teams, where strong relationships can be forged, are a significant part of any leader's success. Hire the best from the very beginning. Look for people with the ability to commit to a bigger cause and who possess values congruent with yours, curiosity and critical thinking skills, common sense, people and relationship skills, risk-taking skills, and respect, admiration, and tolerance for the entrepreneur. Hiring based on these characteristics will result in a team that can identify and implement solutions to the evolving challenges of the legal market today.

*Lawyer Takeaway:* What do you need to do? Well, if you already have mentors and sponsors, thank them. If you are finding that your current team is not helping you strategically, think about people in your network you could develop into mentors and sponsors. As one of our judges shared, however, don't just approach them and say, "Help me!" First, build a relationship with the people you want to approach. Then, approach them with a specific mentoring or sponsoring request. For a prospective mentor at a law firm: "I would really like to find ways to build an independent book of business. I would love to find out what you did that worked and bounce ideas that I have off you from time to time to get your expert perspective." For a prospective sponsor for a future election: "I would really like to run for judge in the next five years. I would love to meet with you to talk about my strategy and find out if you could assist me as I develop my grassroots organization and staff." But don't forget about all those other relationships that you have to develop and nurture. Your colleagues and your network. Your team and your supporters. Relationships are multifaceted and integrate your personal and your professional lives. Your reputation and ability to lead are based both on what you do and who knows you (and what they think about you). One of women's strengths is building relationships and networks. So go get a piece of paper. Write down people you know and what your relationship is with them and where they fall on the scale of these relationships. Seek out relationships in areas where you do not have strengths. Do not forget to build in time to nurture the ones you have. One leader I read about scheduled ninety minutes every week on her calendar to "make calls." She made it a priority to reach out to those in her network.

## TOOT YOUR OWN HORN

*Women need to say to the world: "This is what I'm good at.*
*This is what I can do for you. This is what I'm worth."*
—Patti Wilson, career counselor

*Don't Be Your "First, Worst" Critic*
—Virginia Rometty, CEO, IBM

This section might be more appropriately titled "Visibility" so that people have less of an immediate adverse reaction. At least half of you recoiled when you read that title. People, and women in particular, have a hard time appreciating the difference between acknowledging the contribution they have made to their team and superiors and vainly, cloyingly, self-promoting. We all know women that fly below the radar and never acknowledge their successes, just as we all know women who have a list of their accomplishments at the ready, regardless of whether it is relevant to the conversation. There is a happy medium. Self-deprecation should not serve as the baseline standard, particularly if you want to become a leader in your career and life. Yet there is a way to highlight your successes for the appropriate audience without annoying everyone around you.

In *Secrets of Six-Figure Women*, the author identifies one of the reasons women tend to avoid acknowledging their contributions or skills: "Underlying our unwillingness to speak up is a woman's own inclination to devalue herself. . . . The most salient point about speaking up, as I learned from my interviews, is that you have to consciously and deliberately recognize your worth . . . and make sure others do, too."[65] The book goes on to note that another formula for failure is assuming that others should recognize our talent and know what we want. Many people I spoke with for this book highlighted that being talented will never be enough to get you in positions of leadership. This aspect of ensuring others know of your success dovetails logically with charting your own course: You have to let people know what you want and that you are the right person for the project or position.

There is also an aspect of visibility rolled into this leadership characteristic. Successful women leaders maintain the appropriate amount of visibility. They lead by example and serve as role models for other people. They are intentional about what they say and do, keeping in mind their impact and influence on the world around them. So what you say is intentional and not self-involved. It focuses on the greater goals and accomplishments and the role you play in leading the team to the finish line. Neena Newberry provides a snapshot of how to best create this snapshot of your success:

> Remember that others only see small windows into our accomplishments, **so we have to create an authentic and powerful picture of who we are and how we make a difference.** So, take the time to proactively and consistently share information in a way that's relevant to you and your company—i.e., to provide "strategic snapshots." You never know how others might benefit from your experiences.[66]

One author frames the process as *advocate unabashedly for yourself.*[67] That whole concept of confidence that was key to the risk-taking mentality is also critical to the aspect of speaking up for yourself. You must be confident in your ability and the value you bring to your employer, team, and client in order for your words to be believable. You are just advocating for yourself when you identify your strengths and contributions, just as you likely already do for your family, friends, and team members at work. To achieve your goals, there is always a measure of tooting your own horn: "You must develop your personal business strategy, showcase your strengths, promote your accomplishments and contributions to the business, quantify the value you bring to the business, and strongly advocate for promotions and compensation increases. The most successful women say these are the things they wish they had known earlier in their career."[68] Sometimes half the battle with leading is being able to allow those around you to identify you as a leader.

*Lawyer Takeaway*: Make a list of your contributions at work and on boards and in the community. Make a list of your wins or successes as a lawyer. Make a list of your biggest accomplishments. Then drill it down to a little cheat sheet. Practice telling yourself your successes and leadership skill set. Tell your best friend. You know she won't laugh. Then tell a mentor or sponsor that can help you strengthen the language and perspective. Name the clients you've landed. List the projects you've worked on. Identify the unique skill sets you have—languages, LLMs, pre-law school work history, networks, etc. Be familiar with what makes you such a capable woman practicing law and then be ready to use that in your circles when needed to create or seize opportunities. Also, every time you are chosen for an award or you become a board member for an association or organization, update your résumé. In fact, update your résumé every year even if you haven't had a specific trigger event. That means you will always have it on hand in case someone asks for it, and you will be reminded of your accomplishments and successes when opportunity arises.

## SPEAK UP

*That is what leadership is all about: staking your ground ahead of where opinion is and convincing people, not simply following the popular opinion of the moment.*
—Doris Kearns Goodwin, author and historian

*There is no either/or between being competitive and collaborative. You have to be both and decide which in each situation.*
—Cathie Black, former chairman and president, Hearst Magazines

*There cannot be true democracy unless women's voices are heard.*
—Hillary Rodham Clinton, former First Lady, senator, and secretary of state

**S***peak up* sounds a lot like *toot your own horn*, but it IS different. The latter is more about ensuring people around you acknowledge your contribution. This topic tackles having a voice. Having a seat at the table. Or confronting the issue of "women don't ask," as one book brands it.[69]

In order to develop experience using your voice (if until now you have not used it), practice with small opportunities where the outcome doesn't really matter. I love the following idea and think it is a practical step every woman could use to sharpen her voice: "For example, the next time you're in a store, ask for a discount (and not just because that sweater is missing a button). Practice asking everywhere. The actual discount is not what you're after; it's risk taking. Though it's uncomfortable to do at first, you'll soon get the hang of it."[70] This idea of using your voice, as the authors of *How Remarkable Women Lead* acknowledge, is closely aligned with risk taking. The same fears we discussed in the chapter on risk taking are often the same fears that keep us from using our voice. We refrain from asking, or directing, because of a fear over sounding foolish, being overruled, or not having the best idea.

There is a downside you may confront along the way. In *Secrets of Six-Figure Women*, the author notes, "You're not likely to find much reinforcement for speaking up from the present-day culture, either. According to the Journal of Social Issues, women with a 'directive style' are evaluated more harshly than men. 'I sometimes feel, in meetings, that being direct and straightforward is interpreted as bitchy, whereas from a man it would just be forceful. It's intimidating,' a senior vice president reported. Being cast as a bitch when they're acting confident and bold has even subdued some of the highest earners. Women by nature are relationship-driven."[71] Other books brand this "projecting personal power." This goes beyond being the expert recognized on a topic, but rather having personal power where you show up with confidence, poise, and energy—on the phone, in meetings, giving presentations, interacting with clients, and so on.[72] Speaking up also implicates having that leadership presence of confidence, poise, courage, patience, and ability to manage stress.[73] By knowing when to speak up and how to speak up, your leadership skills will be much more quickly recognized.

I love an example that Sheryl Sandberg shares in *Lean In*—an anecdote to which many lawyer moms can relate. While she ran online sales and operations at Google, Sandberg was expecting a child and was sick during her entire pregnancy. She was parking very far away from the entrance at Google when her husband, then working at Yahoo, pointed out that Yahoo had reserved parking for expectant mothers. She describes how she marched into the Google founder's office and "announced that we needed pregnancy parking, preferably sooner rather than later. He looked up at me and agreed immediately, noting that he had never thought about it before. To this day, I'm embarrassed that I didn't realize that pregnant women needed reserved parking until I experienced my own aching feet. As one of Google's most senior women, didn't I have a special responsibility to think of this? But like Sergey, it has never occurred to me. The other pregnant women must have suffered in silence, not wanting to ask for special treatment. Or maybe they lacked the confidence or seniority to demand that the problem be fixed. Having one pregnant woman at the top made the difference."[74] Sandberg highlights, in this simple example, the many benefits of speaking up. One, you CAN effect change. The change here had never been implemented simply because it had not been considered before. Speaking up often will change things. Two, you can positively impact others. If you are the one who chooses to speak up, then the change that directly impacts you can have a positive ripple effect to others inside, or beyond, the company, firm, or agency where you are.

*Lawyer Takeaway:* If you struggle with speaking up, and not everyone does, then find immediate situations to practice it. Speak up when you are working with a client you know well. Speak up when you're at a cocktail reception. Speak up when you are collaborating in a team meeting with a senior partner or executive. Learn to find your voice. Be persistent. You can never lead if you can't find your voice. But on the flip side, if you often speak up too quickly, learn to moderate your voice so people respect what you have to say. Think before you formulate an opinion and voice it. I know it can be hard in a room full of lawyers who often are heard based on who is the loudest and fastest on their feet, but make sure you can speak up intelligently and that your advice is value added. The more strategic the advice, the more sought-after your counsel will be. Recognize that speaking can effect change, which can result in bettering the circumstances of others as well, so you do need to speak up. Look at the historic lawyers who spoke up and made great strides for all of humanity.

## OTHER TAKEAWAYS

1. **Abandon the Black-and-White Approach/View Success on a Continuum—** How often do we see "success" and "failure" as complete opposites? Something is either a success or it is a failure? Not true. Every time we take a risk and try something new, there will be successful outcomes and also ways to learn and become better the next time around. It's all about your perspective. Let go of the idea that your leadership goals or plans are an all-or-nothing proposition and give yourself some latitude for success as well as learning. In *Break Your Own Rules,* the authors specifically call out this all-or-nothing approach as an old rule that must be left behind and replaced with the new rule Both-And:

Black-and-white thinking does not lead to career success or personal satisfaction. Because complexity and constant change are everywhere in business and in our world today, dealing with ambiguity has become a primary leadership trait that women need to master. One phrase that has crept into dozens of our coaching files over the years is the notion of having it all. It's no coincidence that many of the women who are trying to have it all are also the ones who are most disappointed and frustrated. This is just one example of the type of extreme thinking that pushes us off the path to success.[75]

This is highlighted in the following quote from Susan Ivey, CEO of Reynolds American, "The equation to solve for is happiness with the least amount of guilt. There are no right answers here."[76]

2. **Persistence**—Jane Goodall once said, "If you really want something, and really work hard, and take advantage of opportunities, and never give up, you will find a way." I have read and heard repeatedly about women at the top of our field saying that they got knocked down, didn't win an election or a promotion or a project, but they just kept going. They learned something from the hit they took, but they didn't agonize by constantly looking in the rearview mirror at the defeat. They moved on knowing they had a greater purpose and a bigger goal. Persistence. Stick-to-it-ness. Courage. Decisiveness. All words that describe a great leader. In *How Women Lead*, the authors describe how persistence actually equates to taking charge of your own destiny: "Self-confident women are persistent. If one approach does not work, they develop another way to achieve the goal. In pursuit of an important goal, they have the courage to continue forward no matter the odds."[77]

3. **Take Care of Yourself**—It can be easiest to put your needs lowest in the priority order because you are the easiest to ignore. It's hard to set aside a demanding client, team member, supervisor, or even a child, but your welfare can easily be moved to the back of the line. Not to mention that many women see "self-care" as selfish. Yet without allocating time to relax and replenish, you can find yourself on the fast track to career burnout. As a leader it is critical to set an example for your team that there is more to life

than your career. If you model the behavior for your team, then they will be more likely to follow it in their own lives, and you will find you have a healthier, more fulfilled team working on your behalf. Additionally, calendaring downtime leaves you with time to get to know yourself. Unless you connect to yourself regularly, you can't expect others to know you.

When leaders were asked by a *Forbes Magazine* author what they needed to improve, they frequently responded that they needed to take better care of themselves. The author explains why: "If you don't take care of *you*, then how can you take care of your team or organization? The answer is not simply about health and fitness, though that is part of the equation. It is more about taking time to know yourself."[78] This piece of advice can run long on platitudes and short on practical tips, so here are three from a leadership skills article: (1) You may have to set some limits with people in your life, making sure they understand that you are truly committed to good self-care. (2) Don't allow yourself to be talked out of your self-care needs. Establish a routine and stick to it. (3) Give good self-care even during a crisis or stressful time. After all, that's when you'll need it the most.[79]

As Jane Fraser of Citigroup counsels, "When I leave at night, it's done. I shut down. I find I need some time with no voices to relax. I call that my recovery time. I detox and get the stress out by having quiet for a while."[80]

# 5

# Insight from the Top

## Interviews with Legal Leaders

*Find out who you are and do it on purpose.*
　　　　—Dolly Parton, singer-songwriter, author, and actress

*Knowing that we can make a difference in this world is a great motivator. How can we know this and not be involved?*
　　　　—Susan Jeffers, author and speaker

*Don't let anything stop you. There will be times when you'll be disappointed, but you can't stop. Make yourself the very best that you can make of what you are. The very best.*
　　　　—Sadie T. Alexander, first woman law school graduate,
　　　　first African American woman to earn a PhD in economics

■ ■ ■

Who could have better, more real-world perspective on what it takes to lead, and how to overcome those pesky obstacles, than those women in law who have led their way straight to the top? Six straight-talking successes, who have also suffered their share of disappointments and challenges, have offered their insight on what it takes to lead successfully and persevere through the dark times.

57

From the CEO of a nonprofit to a US senator and from the marble floors of financial institutions to the carpeted halls of a major law firm, these women received their law degrees at different times and in different places, but all faced similar challenges. They struck out on different paths, but each reached the pinnacle of her career (though they are not done yet!) through risk taking, perseverance, optimism, and, gasp, even listening.

I asked these inspirational six a handful of questions and let them select what they wanted to cover. The questions included:

- What leadership technique do you most admire?
- What was the greatest challenge you had to overcome and how did you tackle it?
- What piece of advice would you give women starting out in the law who want to make a mark on the legal profession and their community?
- What female leader inspired you?
- What is the best leadership characteristic to cultivate?
- Do you have a favorite quote you use or love?

See if their paths and choices resonate in your own aspirations in the pages that follow, and I dare you not to be inspired to action as you hear their voices urging us on.

**Marina Park**
CEO, Girl Scouts of Northern California
*Learn to actively listen.*

**M**arina Park has been named one of the most influential women in business in the Bay Area for five years running. As CEO of Girl Scouts of Northern California, Ms. Park has led the post-merger transformation of five Girl Scout councils into one, delivering services to 47,000 girls and 32,000 adult members across nineteen counties. Ms. Park joined Girl Scouts after twenty-five years of leading in private practice because she believes in the Girl Scouts' mission: to build girls of courage, confidence, and character who make the world a better place. In her private practice career, Ms. Park served as the managing partner of the first woman-led major law firm in the United States. She was elected to three successive terms as managing partner and negotiated and implemented two of the largest law firm mergers in the United States as part of a four-person management team. Ms. Park also established a diversity program that earned top rankings from *Working Mother* and other national publications. Remarkably, with all of these leadership achievements, the first thing I learned listening to Marina Park is that she does a fair amount of listening herself.

Ms. Park shared with us insight into the leadership skill that she most admires:

*Everyone needs to develop the ability to listen—truly listen. We each have our own ideas and opinions constantly rolling through our minds. But an effective leader cultivates the talent of being an active listener rather than thinking about how he or she is going to respond when the person opposite stops talking. Be quiet and truly take in what they are saying. Let them know that you are listening to what they have to say and understand that you actually appreciate their insight and perspective. Model that listening skill constantly for others in the organization you lead or work for.*

Ms. Park served in private practice at an Am Law 100 firm for twenty-five years, where she says this active listening skill can be the most elusive. She highlights how listening can be particularly hard in legal organizations, or for that matter in any big organization, because, "we find ourselves so passionate about what we believe is important and then focus on persuading others to win them over to our way of seeing or doing something. But we are not all right, all the time, and any one of us does not have all the answers." Ms. Park even notes the intrinsic challenge for women practicing law because women have learned that we have to interject in order to be heard. She understands that women may need to be prepared to jump into the conversation when opportunity arises, but she urges not to do so at the expense of listening. She cautions women seeking to lead effectively not to be "so prepared" to jump into any conversation break that we spend all our time thinking about what we are going to say instead of appreciating the insight from the speaker. That means being mindful of active listening, and Ms. Park advises:

> *Understand how and why this benefits you as the leader, and catch yourself when you are not actively listening to the speaker. If you are leading a group or a team, and you have set out to make it an effective group, then spend time telling the group about the importance of listening. Both modeling listening before the group and giving them the permission and an opportunity to "call each other on it" when they fail to listen can maximize the effectiveness and engagement of the group. Create time for group members to think about what has been said instead of requiring an instant response. Building quiet time to process and reflect into group sessions also makes a more inviting environment for the participants to truly listen to the speaker since they know they will have time to formulate a response. Additionally, meetings where the particpants are actively listening create an environment where people want to spend time. If your group or team members feel like they are going to be heard, and people know they are being listened to when they speak, then they want to come to the meeting. Wouldn't you be more likely to appreciate someone engaging you if they took the time to ask you the questions and appreciate your perspective? Most significantly, you are much more likely to have the full support of your team after the decision is reached. The team feels like they had a stake in coming up with the solution. They were heard and good reasons by smart people were given, and therefore the team members will "buy in" to the path forward and support it within the*

*larger organization. This can be a very hard and threatening thing to do as a woman practicing law. But it is an invaluable leadership skill.*

When asked what leadership quality she finds most useful as a CEO of a non-profit organization, Ms. Park said that the ability to dive deeply into the details without getting stuck there has been a critical skill set in her role here and elsewhere. Ms. Park mentioned that often there is a perception that leaders must serve as the "big picture" people rather than people who involve themselves in the details. However, her ability to move between the big picture and the details informs her even more accurately about the plans and paths of the organization she leads: "Absolutely you must rise above the details and synthesize the issues across the organization. A leader must be able to see around corners. You have to anticipate what might be happening, and look down the road, but then let that big picture knowledge inform what you bring back to the detailed issues you are working on at present. Being able to move in and out of different levels and depths within an organization has proved to be an invaluable resource for me."

Finally, Ms. Park closed our time together by saying that one of the most helpful tools she has in her leadership tool kit is the ability to stay calm in the midst of a storm. Ironically, she learned this skill as a teenager by actually staying calm in the middle of storms. Ms. Park grew up racing sailboats with her dad. She recalled a particularly harrowing storm they found themselves battling on board their sailboat with the crew. Even though some on the boat were injured, her father calmly called out orders and engendered both respect and action from those around him, which enabled them to weather the storm and save the boat and the crew. Ms. Park wisely counsels:

*No one will have faith in a leader who is fearful, chaotic, or panicked in the midst of a crisis. The reality is, the leader must do what has to be done and give people the confidence that you know what is going on and the ship is not sinking. You must cultivate the ability to settle people down, focus on what needs to get done, and then do it. Remaining calm will give those around you the confidence that you are in control and things will turn out okay, and that in turn will engender action and trust.*

Now that's a captain we can all get behind.

**Diane C. Yu**
Chief of Staff and Deputy to the President,
New York University
*Hold on to your hopes and your dreams and your ideals.*

If she sounds like she knows what she's talking about, it's because she does. Diane C. Yu has taught leadership classes at New York University for eleven years. Her résumé is impressive: private practice after law school, appointed by the president as a White House Fellow, general counsel for the State Bar of California, California Superior Court commissioner, associate general counsel at Monsanto Company, and now chief of staff and deputy to the president at New York University. But it's her insight into leadership that will blow you away.

First, if nothing else, Ms. Yu is honest about leadership. She cautions:

*It's difficult. Leadership is a challenge for your intellectual resources, for your interpersonal relationships, for your emotional well-being. Because you have to take risks, you have to make the decisions, you have to do things that are unpopular or not understood, you have to deal with criticism and people who are disappointed. Leadership is continually assailed with complex problems that require a great deal of resilience. Leadership requires self-confidence. Self-awareness. A positive attitude about life; leadership is always easiest if you have a positive attitude. Leading can be lonely; rewarding and fulfilling and exciting but also lonely. Among the most lonely times are those when you have made the decision, which you had to make, but which others are scrutinizing. Some people see leadership as having power and moving people, but you have to deal with competing claims that can be equally compelling, and your decisions will be met with resistance. A leader needs persuasion to be successsful. People underestimate the difficulties, the strain, the pain that all accompany rising to the top.*

After that realistic assessment for women aspiring to lead, Ms. Yu still encourages you to aspire to leadership because you can improve the situation or circumstances of many people: "That's what drives you. To make things better. To forge a path for others to follow." She reminds us that we cannot blindly enter into leadership roles without a practical perspective of what that leadership comes with, yet the burden is one we must bear in order to effect change and make a positive difference in the world around us.

Ms. Yu urges women in leadership roles to retain their hopes and ideals and dreams. The *sweet spot* of an effective leader, she shares, is a woman "with a sense of integrity, personal character, and values which are consistent with how you are performing as a leader. In that leader, there is no jarring conflict. There is no collision of views and values. **Be who you are.**"

A woman who leads can obtain the confidence and trust of others, Ms. Yu advises. The clearest feedback on whether you are a leader is if people are willing to say, *We believe in your ideas and personal character and ability, and we're willing to be on your team*. She continues that a leader must have the ability to enlist followers, allies, and partners in order to get something done. Successful leaders have made change. The change may be a result of you inspiring it, leading the charge, or motivating it, but Ms. Yu shares that something **must** change for you to be a leader. Leading is not for planners who don't act on their plans.

In discussing the legal field specifically, she highlights that women are intellectually and academically and professionally every bit the equal of men, but in some areas women still lag behind. In surveying who occupies leadership roles in the law, this is evident, and Ms. Yu encourages women not to be hesitant to lead because of an unwillingness to put themselves out there or concern over creating resentment or envy. Even if you feel you have been beaten down after taking a risk, or have concern over continuing bias and stereotypes that pose extra obstacles that make leadership a more difficult enterprise, women must still step up and step into the fray. Ms. Yu acknowledges that as long as the career-building years and the child-rearing years clash, it will be extremely hard to make rapid progress. "There has to be a better system and set of timing priorities and principles that incorporate flexibility."

If required to give a list of skills critical in successful leadership, Ms. Yu lays out the following top three list:

*Number One: Have a vision, ambition, or aspiration. It excites people.*

*Number Two: Work well with people. Listen, collaborate, synthesize competing views, and develop a path forward or out. You must be able to explain the plan to those who aren't on board in order to get them on board. Be persuasive. Make people feel valued, and do not use them as tools for your own glory.*

*Number Three: Have a sense of who you are. Possess self-awareness and criticism, not overmuch as some of us are prone, and a clear sense of values without being intolerant. There's an "integrity" package, which means you are worthy of trust because you are trustworthy. Know generally which direction you lead and what your values are. Do not be a cipher who is mysterious and unknowable—the worst leader is an unpredictable one because there is no stable ground.*

Beyond all that, Ms. Yu maintains, just have some patience and persistence. The reality is that you could fail once or a million times. Scientists do a million lab tests before getting to the answer. She shares a quote from Margot Fonteyn that she uses in her leadership classes: "The one important thing I have learned over the years is the difference between taking one's work seriously and taking one's self seriously. The first is imperative and the second is disastrous."

In a moment of personal insight, Ms. Yu shares, "When the obstacle makes me feel insecure—I have to turn and look at the problem, and not at myself and how I feel about it. I have a better shot at solving the problem if I don't make it personal. You can't get so consumed with your own needs and insecurities that those worries get in the way of leading effectively. Recognize when you are overwhelmed, take a few deep breaths, tackle the problem, and don't focus on yourself. We all make the worst decisions in moments of insecurity and moments of panic. Call out, as President Lincoln urged, to the better angels of our nature."

That's a reminder that would serve us all well.

**Janet L. McDavid**
Partner, Hogan Lovells
*Have a vision of what you want to achieve.*

Janet L. McDavid leads with the punchline. If she sounds like she knows how to get to the point, it's because she has made a career of successfully communicating—to colleagues, to clients, to adversaries, and to judges. In what's becoming a rarity in legal circles these days, Ms. McDavid joined her firm, Hogan Lovells, in Washington, DC, thirty-nine years ago after graduating from Georgetown Law School and has been with them ever since. She has led in her firm, as co-leader of its Antitrust, Competition, and Economic Regulation practice; in the bar, including service as chair of the ABA Section of Antitrust Law; in government, providing transition advice on the Federal Trade Commission to the Obama, Bush, and Clinton administrations; and in speaking, writing, and community service. Ms. McDavid not only has a reputation for her legal skills but also for her practical wisdom. *Who's Who Legal* named her "one of the finest antitrust lawyers around" and lauded her for "very good judgment and practical advice," which she shares with us here. *Effective leaders have a vision of what they want to achieve. They each have different styles to get there, but they all have incredible organizational skills and they really think about how to take an issue forward. Some of my friends and colleagues will make the decision about what they want to achieve, and then they set out doing it in a very single-minded way.*

Ms. McDavid has had her share of obstacles in becoming a leading antitrust lawyer. She laughingly shares the advice a friend of hers gave her when she was up against similar obstacles: "Use parent effectiveness training in the office just as you would at home. Whenever you are dealing with a difficult individual, parrot what you learned to do as a mom, 'I know you are angry and I hear what you are saying. . . .' It works."

But it's more than just that active listening technique Ms. McDavid says women leaders possess. They are inclusive in their leadership, she shares. "Female leaders often seek input and work very collaboratively—men are much more singular in their leadership styles."

One of the critical skills her own firm develops in younger lawyers is hands-on practice. More than just "training," young lawyers are placed on teams, even if they are small administrative teams, where they can practice leading. Junior associates may be given the opportunity to manage a team of support personnel, summer associates, or contract lawyers on a project in order to understand what works effectively. There's no substitute for actually leading, even if you make mistakes, Ms. McDavid says. "As attorneys take on management and leadership of a small project, they will gradually be able to take on more significant projects. I believe that holding an actual leadership role is critical to a lawyer's development." Practice makes perfect—or at least improved.

When asked what lawyers should do if their current work environment does not encourage, or even allow, such hands-on leadership practice, Ms. McDavid urges lawyers to find ways to develop such opportunities. For example, the ABA is one such mechanism where lawyers can grow into leadership by doing. First, she recommends, volunteer to take on a project for a committee or section. *If you deliver on a project, then you will rise like cream to the top of the leadership barrel. So often, attorneys just fail to deliver. If you can prove yourself able to follow through, then you will be given even greater opportunities. Make the most of that. Deliver.* After you have proven your capability and commitment, next you have to seize the leadership opportunities that become available.

In addition to the concept of practice makes perfect when it comes to leadership, mentorship is a critical component in developing as a lawyer, Ms. McDavid notes. Mentors are men and women who are on your side and provide perspective, wisdom, and guidance when you are confronted with a given obstacle or opportunity.

*Mentor relationships cannot be forced. They develop naturally from friendships or working relationships. Additionally, mentor relationships change over time.* Expect that and don't plan on one set of mentors/supporters as being the right fit for each stage of your career, as Ms. McDavid has experienced personally. You have to enjoy working with your mentor and have a "spark" to connect you. She shares that people who at one point may have been your mentors, may soon enough become your equals. And she strongly encourages lawyers not to "pull the ladder up after them." As you grow and develop, it is critical that you become a mentor to those who come after you. In the legal arena, she has seen people fail to give back after people have generously mentored them. Ms. McDavid said that people who have succeeded at her firm connect and support and communicate with those from the very "top of the heap to the bottom."

Ms. McDavid's recommendations to have a vision of what you want, practice leadership to become good at leading, and develop relationships with key people who will mentor and develop you are the building blocks not only for her own career but also for a successful legal career for anyone with a goal to lead in their field.

**Suzanne Nora Johnson**
Former Vice Chairman, The Goldman Sachs
Group, Inc.
*Inspire those around you.*

S uzanne Nora Johnson's résumé reads like something out of leadership storybooks. Ms. Johnson was vice chairman of Goldman Sachs, chairman of the Global Markets Institute, head of the firm's Global Investment Research Division, and a member of the firm's Management Committee. She joined Goldman Sachs in 1985 and became a partner in 1992. Prior to joining the firm, she held a federal judicial clerkship and positions in a prestigious firm. Ms. Johnson has served, and currently serves, on prominent corporate and philanthropic boards. She earned her JD from Harvard Law School and her BA from the University of Southern California. She has been ranked by *Forbes* at number 34 on its list of "The World's 100 Most Powerful Women."

Ms. Johnson shared that one of the most critical leadership tactics is, in times of adversity, to provide the people around you with inspiration, the tools to move forward, and the drive to get to a better place. A true leader must possess the vision and the strategy to guide the team or company to the successful end goal. In Ms. Johnson's approach, that does not mean sugarcoating the circumstances. She encourages people trying to lead in the midst of challenges:

> *You have to paint a realistic and pragmatic picture for the people involved with assisting you to achieve the outcome. But then you must inspire them. The inspiration is what will move your team forward. An effective leader continually communicates the end goals both to the larger group, through self-reinforcing messaging, as well as communicating the message to individuals where the message can be customized to each team member's specific strengths and weaknesses to make it most effective.*

On the subject of whether a leader should focus on the "big picture" or the details, Ms. Johnson is clear that a leader must do both. She emphasizes, "The best leaders understand the details and are conversant with them. However, they must then delegate the tasks of executing and operating to people they trust so they can focus on the big picture issues. A leader cannot be so far removed from the specifics that they are unable to offer pragmatic advice and can only offer unhelpful platitudes." This ability to move seamlessly between the larger, broader end goals and the specifics of the day-to-day application is a message that unites Ms. Johnson with many of the successful women leading globally today.

If you face obstacles, then give people your ideas for "work-arounds," She urges. "There is no straight line to an end goal," Ms. Johnson reminds aspiring leaders. Rather, there must continually be work-arounds developed to circumvent the obstacle from overcoming the vision or goal. Ms. Johnson emphasizes that a successful leader also encourages and cultivates certain characteristics, in herself and her team: "Encourage creativity. Encourage persistence. Persistence and stamina are the most important factors to have. Half of success is hanging in there." It is that persistence and creativity that enable people to problem-solve and come up with resourceful solutions. Ms. Johnson shares that a leader must give people the charge, communicate it effectively, and then provide positive reinforcement when they come up with a solution to the trial that works.

When asked what piece of advice she would share with a new lawyer just beginning her career, Ms. Johnson says the best advice is to communicate. Leaders not only communicate their vision, but they also understand and adopt the vision of those leading them. She shares:

*Make sure you have strong lines of communication up the chain as well as down the chain. Talk collaterally. Stretch yourself and move beyond the weeds. It's easy to stay mired down in the minutia as you begin your career, but women must move beyond the details even at the beginning. Communicate your accomplishments. Additionally, have discussions about your challenges without framing them as your weaknesses. Do not equate a challenge you face to a weakness you possess. One way to successfully differentiate between the two is to make sure that you are doing more than reporting information factually. Women are good at reporting facts, but you must give color commentary and nuance. Outline the facts, but then provide takeaways to the recipients of your communication. Similarly, you could just provide the message from the outset, and then just use the facts as the backup to your message.*

Framing the messaging, communicating the vision, and weathering the storms through an inspirational message have set Suzanne Nora Johnson apart as a successful and effective leader. And it's that advice, to communicate effectively, that can improve all of our leadership abilities.

**Carrie Hightman**
Executive Vice President and
Chief Legal Officer, NiSource Inc.
*Notice how to inspire people.*

She always knew what she wanted. In a way many graduates leaving law school do not. Carrie Hightman's résumé reflects her ambition. Prior to joining NiSource, she served as president of AT&T Illinois. In that position, she was responsible for all regulatory, legislative, governmental, and external affairs activities, as well as community and industry relations, throughout Illinois. Prior to joining AT&T, Ms. Hightman was a partner in the Chicago law firm of Schiff Hardin, where she led its Energy, Telecommunications, and Public Utilities practice group. She began her career in the public sector in 1983, serving in-house at the Florida Public Service Commission and then as associate counsel at the Florida Office of Public Counsel. She was appointed chair of the fifteen-member Illinois Board of Higher Education by the governor of Illinois and serves on numerous other organizations in Chicago and nationwide.

In talking with Ms. Hightman, you can sense her vision and the direction that guided her from an early stage in her career when she recognized an emerging growth opportunity in the legal field in Florida and changed jobs to become an expert in the area. She even quotes Margaret Thatcher when emphasizing how important a sense of purpose is: "If you have a sense of purpose and a sense of direction, I believe people will follow you." And like other women we talked to, Ms. Hightman also laughingly acknowledges that you can't very well lead without followers. That sense of direction is critical to amassing them. She notes an important distinction, though—just being a manager or supervisor or boss does NOT make you a leader. You may have people that have to listen to you because of your position, but that does not translate to leading successfully. A different skill set is necessary.

Ms. Hightman not only talks the leadership talk, but she walks the leadership walk. She spends considerable energy encouraging those up-and-coming women to develop necessary leadership skill sets, and she even developed Building the NextGen, which set out to recruit, develop, and retain women at

NiSource. She meets annually with both leaders and women aspiring to lead to encourage them, and she shared in her interview the five leadership characteristics she highlighted as "must-haves" for those women: authenticity, observation, self-awareness, humility, and intentionality.

Authenticity, she acknowledges, is a buzzword in leadership circles these days, but being yourself is a critical component to becoming an effective leader. Observation you hear less about, however. Ms. Hightman counsels:

> *Carefully observe leaders you come in contact with and learn from their examples—both good and bad. Take note of how managers inspire (or fail to inspire) the people around them. Watch how (and if) they delegate responsibilities. And observe how they approach new opportunities to lead. You'll probably learn as much from your bad bosses as from your good ones. Indeed, sometimes the most important leadership lesson is learning what not to do. A great example of that is a former boss that was ineffective. She was constantly in panic mode, which put her team constantly on edge. She lacked confidence in herself, which drained the confidence from her direct reports. Her style created confusion and disarray. People want leaders who are confident, have a great strategy, give clear direction, and then support their team's execution. Teams need to believe their bosses have confidence not only in themselves, but also in what their teams are doing. My observations showed me what not to do when leading a team.*

Ms. Hightman continues, saying that self-awareness is also an oft-overlooked skill. You must understand how others see you and modify your style and behavior as necessary to improve your impact (without sacrificing who you are in the process). If you are self-aware, you know your strengths and development needs, and you can adjust your behavior. Accept that development is a continuous process and that regardless of whether you are just starting out as a leader or are well into your leadership path, there is always room for improvement.

Ms. Hightman shared a personal story to illustrate how humility can be a critical component in a leader:

> *A good leader knows that he or she doesn't have every answer. Indeed, the best leaders know well what they don't know and surround themselves with a team that can fill those gaps. Humility is an essential trait to effective lead-*

*ership. But one of the most common mistakes that leaders make is failing to embrace this fact. When I think about this characteristic, I think about my favorite boss before coming to NiSource. I couldn't put my finger on what set him apart from other bosses until the night of his retirement party. He left the company after thirty-plus years, and we had a wonderful dinner with his direct reports and their spouses. There were about thirty people in the room. At the end of the dinner, before dessert, we planned to present him with a gift, but he had a different plan. Before we could even start the presentation, he got up and told a special story about each of his direct reports and then proceeded to provide each of us a framed copy of what he said about us. He was retiring, but he gave each of us a gift. He didn't talk about his career, but instead he focused on what he gained from each of us. There was not a dry eye in the room. It was the best demonstration of humility by a leader that I had ever seen, and it exemplified his powerfully effective leadership style.*

Finally, Ms. Hightman emphasizes intentionality, or taking ownership of your career and being strategic about it. Don't simply allow your career to happen to you, She warns, "Take charge of it and make it what you want it to be. Set your own agenda. Be intentional about the jobs you take and the ones you turn down. Look for positions or assignments that take you in the direction you want to go or help you develop skills you need to achieve your career end game. Importantly, be prepared and willing to seize opportunities, despite risks. Also, once you figure out the things that make you most effective, do them deliberately and regularly. Lead on purpose."

That's the encouragement we all need as we set our sights on stepping up our leadership potential: Be deliberate and lead on purpose!

**Mazie K. Hirono**
US Senator (D-Hawaii)
*Develop relationships wherever you are.*

Senator Mazie K. Hirono is the first Asian American woman ever elected to the US Senate, and her journey to the top is an inspirational story of a leader who came from humble beginnings and overcame difficult obstacles. Born in Japan, she spent her early years on her grandparents' rice farm and at age eight left Japan with her mother and brother in search of a better life. Constantly working, she found her way to the University of Hawaii and then to Georgetown Law School. After returning to Hawaii, she practiced law, served as a state legislator, Hawaii lieutenant governor, and US representative. She won her US Senate seat in 2012, defeating a candidate against whom she had previously run and lost. Senator Hirono knows the importance of never burning bridges and overcoming daunting challenges.

When asked about a leadership skill she has found most useful, the senator emphasizes collaboration:

> It's important to develop relationships with others and work in a collaborative and cooperative way. You spend time getting to know someone, sharing stories, and building trust. You may not all come from the same background— for example, I don't come from a middle-class background—but you find common ground. In the political arena there is less time available to develop those opportunities, so seize them when the chance arises.

Senator Hirono knows about challenges. She spoke openly about her numerous political races and the unique challenges each one of them brought. One example she shared was her race for governor. She worked tirelessly on the campaign but lost despite her best efforts. While losses are hard, Senator Hirono shared that she just kept going and never gave up. Additionally, she spent time reflecting. She reviewed and assessed her campaign after the loss and decided that next time she would ensure she ran a modern campaign with a fresh perspective. Senator Hirono shared what we all must be reminded of when we don't first achieve what we sought out to achieve. "Dust yourself off and get back up," the senator urges. "But learn something from the defeat. Allow the loss to provide you with perspective that makes you stronger, so you can succeed the next time you dare to run the race, take the test, or seek the promotion."

Senator Hirono felt strongly that she wanted to serve her state of Hawaii, and so she pressed on to the next race and the next opportunity. The senator shared:

*I have wanted to give back for a long time. And I knew what I was fighting for. But to succeed, you also have to approach the challenge with a practical list of what it will take to succeed. There are three things that are critical in a race: You must have resources, you must have a strategy, a team of people who know how to win and that you can respect, and you must have wide grassroots support. I have learned practicality is critical. Determination is necessary.*

Early in her journey she never thought she would run for office. As an immigrant child with little means, she was not raised around politics. However, the senator shared how critical the encouragement of other women is for their success. Role models over the course of her leadership development played a significant role in her growth. As a result, Senator Hirono is now actively involved in supporting women who run for office. She knows women supporting women yields results, and there are not currently enough women holding political office. One of the benefits of women in public service is women's ability to work collaboratively, which she says is key in politics.

The woman Senator Hirono most admires is her mother. She said that her mother could teach us all about leadership. When her mother set out to escape an abusive husband in her native country, she showed that one person can make a difference. And that's the truth, the senator reminds us. When her mother faced innumerable obstacles in a new land with a new language and no resources, she demonstrated fierce determination and an attitude that she would never give up. Determination is required of any leader. When her mother set out into the unknown to make a better life, she showed an unwavering courage and ability to risk it all. The senator emphasizes that risk taking is a must for successful leadership.

In her closing remarks, Senator Hirono shared the quotation that motivates her as a leader. Dr. Martin Luther King once stated, "The arc of the moral universe is long but it bends towards justice." Because of her life experiences, Senator Hirono firmly believes that it is justice that guides her and inspires her to lead. Justice does not occur on its own. Justice requires willing leaders to ensure its execution. And Senator Hirono is seeking to do just that.

# 6

# View from the Bench

## Interviews with the Judiciary

*Yes, I will bring the understanding of a woman to the Court, but I doubt that alone will affect my decisions. I think the important thing about my appointment is not that I will decide cases as a woman, but that I am a woman who will get to decide cases.*
　　　—Sandra Day O'Connor, first female US Supreme Court justice

*Doubt yourself and you doubt everything you see. Judge yourself and you see judges everywhere. But if you listen to the sound of your own voice, you can rise above doubt and judgment. And you can see forever.*
　　　　　　　　　　　　　　　　—Nancy Lopez, professional golfer

■■■

Judges have a unique perspective of what it takes to effectively lead. They see women first-chair trials. They see women lead bar associations. They see women head the school fundraising drive, preside over charitable boards, and bravely write dissenting opinions. And fortunately, a few remarkable and diverse women serving in America's judiciary today, from both federal and state courts, have agreed to share their thoughts on the best characteristics a woman in the legal field today can cultivate to lead inside and outside the courtroom. We have an entire chapter highlighting women in the judiciary because of this unique perspective they bring to legal leadership and their willingness to share it.

But as you will see, these judges offer more than just a judicial perspective on leadership. They ***are*** leading women in the law. They lead beyond the courtroom. And they have led in careers prior to achieving their position on the bench. In fact, many began cutting their leadership teeth in undergraduate and law school when they saw change that needed to happen. They have led private law firms. They have led in government and politics. They have held leading roles in corporations, with nonprofits, on boards, in associations, and in education.

So I asked these fabulous five the same questions I asked our "Insight from the Top" leaders and saw many of the same themes on leadership emerge. What works before the bench works beyond it as well.

From sea to shining sea, these leading members of America's judiciary counsel us to garner respect, take risks, stay confident, develop relationships, and break our own internal glass ceilings. Let their words inspire you and educate you as you chart your own leadership course.

**Judge Jennifer Walker Elrod**
US Court of Appeals for the Fifth Circuit
*Set your own timetable.*

If you hadn't seen her résumé, then you would feel like you were sitting down to have coffee with a girlfriend. From Harvard Law School to judicial clerkships to a successful career at an Am Law 100 firm, Judge Jennifer Walker Elrod has found success at every turn. But she also frankly shared that her path was not without disappointment. Among the several pieces of wisdom on leadership she had to offer, Judge Elrod shared a compelling conversation she had with a colleague after a disappointing loss during the appointment process. He looked at her, after she had been passed over for a state district court bench, and said, "Why are you letting other people determine *your* timetable? If you really want to serve on the bench, run for judge."

It is that take-charge, risk-taking approach that has led Judge Elrod into positions of leadership and success. When she was appointed to the US Court of Appeals for the Fifth Ciruit, Judge Elrod became the youngest woman sitting on the federal appellate bench. She shared these encouraging words to consider if at first we don't succeed:

> When I ran for judge, it was not a good "business" decision. I was a senior associate. I needed to bill hours. Someone signed up to run against me in the primaries. But I was so thoroughly invested in serving as a member of the judiciary that I jumped and took the risk. You have to be willing to lose and fail and embarrass yourself. I was passed over for two state district bench nominations before I ran for judge. It is not over if you "lose" or "fail." I learned something through each of those periods. I learned more about people and the system and how much I really wanted it. There is life after defeat. Sometimes, it is an even better life than had you never taken the risk.

Judge Elrod encourages women practicing today to realize they can achieve anything they set out to accomplish, but they must believe they are good enough.

To illustrate her point, she shared a story about a woman who attended a conference where she recently spoke. Judge Elrod told the conference attendees about a recent study showing that far fewer women apply for judicial clerkships than men. Then she reached into her desk to show me a letter she had just received from a law student attendee. The woman wrote Judge Elrod saying she had decided just before the conference that she would not apply for a judicial clerkship, though she wanted one, because she believed she was not accomplished enough to find a position. After the conference, she reconsidered, applied for a position, and won a federal clerkship position for next fall. Judge Elrod commented, "Had she never applied, she would always have wondered. Regardless of what the outcome is, go after what you want. Take the risk."

Judge Elrod also shared that great mentors were one of the key components to her ability to lead and succeed. Even in her earliest legal job, as a clerk for a federal judge, she found mentor relationships helped her develop an understanding of the law and navigate her career. After Judge Elrod left her clerkship, her judge continued to serve as a sounding board as well as a source of information and solid advice. Along the way, she sought out people whose judgment she trusted and developed mentoring relationships to help her learn and grow. Her mentors were not only women—in fact, her early mentors were men. They helped her understand and navigate the legal field, as she had not grown up in a family of lawyers.

Mentor relationships do not just develop on the first day, Judge Elrod cautions: "Be honest about what you need. Don't approach a prospective mentor on the first day asking to be mentored. Do good work. Once you have done good work, you will earn the opportunity to develop a mentoring relationship because it will benefit you and it will benefit the mentor to grow the talent of someone on his or her team."

On being a mentor, Judge Elrod encourages women to surround themselves with a strong team: "Hire good people. Trust their judgment. Give them responsibility. You cannot go beyond a certain point without having a team you can delegate to in order to expand your opportunities. Once you have exceptional people, support and train them. Even when there are mistakes, use those as opportunities to teach the team."

Finally, Judge Elrod shares that sometimes lawyers can find themselves paralyzed by the choices:

*You cannot do everything for everyone in every area of your life in every season. You make the choices. You decide what works for you now. Your decision now does not prevent you from making different choices at a different time. Both Margaret Thatcher and Justice O'Connor had to leave the workforce for family reasons at one point, but upon returning to work they enjoyed incredible professional success.*

My favorite story Judge Elrod shared was at the close of our meeting. Judge Elrod has two daughters, one who was in preschool when she began serving in the judiciary. Judge Elrod also has a number of women friends her daughters know who also serve as judges. During preschool share time one day, the teacher asked each child what they wanted to be when they grew up. Her daughter's classmate, a boy, said he wanted to be a judge. Judge Elrod's daughter quickly retorted, "You can't be a judge. Judges are girls!"

Judge Elrod is not only leading on the bench and in the legal community, but she is also showing the next generation of women that "judges are girls!"

**Judge Ann Claire Williams**
US Court of Appeals for the Seventh Circuit
*Never give up.*

Judge Anne Claire Williams is a trailblazer. When appointed, she was the first African American judge on the US Court of Appeals for the Seventh Circuit, as she was on her federal district bench before that. She has worked in jobs as diverse as elementary school music teacher to assistant US attorney. Despite all her awards and recognitions for forging new trails and leading, Judge Williams speaks with the highest regard for the trailblazers that preceded her. The most critical leadership tool that Judge Williams emphasized is mentoring. While everyone we spoke with mentioned the mentors that helped them as they developed, Judge Williams described her profound mentoring relationships in great detail and said that mentoring was a central component of her success in developing as a lawyer, judge, and leader. She described lessons learned from two of her mentors specifically: Constance Baker Motley, the first African American woman ever to sit on a federal district court bench, and Betty Fletcher, who presided on the US Court of Appeals for the Ninth Circuit until she passed away in 2012.

She shared personal stories of her "tremendous mentor," Judge Motley, and how she had constantly faced the perception in the courtroom that she wasn't good enough. Judge Williams recounts Judge Motley's time at the Legal Defense Fund with Thurgood Marshall when she was placed in harm's way. Judge Motley's charge to Judge Williams was that she had to learn to laugh at things and not carry a chip on her shoulder. The four "Be's" that Judge Williams recounts from her mentorship relationship with Judge Motley are:

- Be strong.
- Be strategic.
- Be wise.
- Be determined. (Never give up!)

There was much wisdom Judge Williams gleaned from Judge Motley that inspired her to lead. She related how Judge Motley helped her understand that you have to keep your eye on the prize despite obstacles that might arise: "All the New York clubs were male only and all the judges used to go for their monthly meetings. She [Motley] noticed that she was able to go to the meetings and wondered how she got in—turned out, the other judges told the club she was their secretary in order to gain her admittance." Judge Motley's perseverance encouraged Judge Williams's own. Judge Williams continued, "She was also married and had a son and was totally devoted to family. That mentoring relationship showed me how to master juggling, but it also taught me that you can be professional, have the respect of peers, and also have a family and be feminine." Judge Williams reflects that Judge Fletcher also showed her that family and successfully leading are not mutually exclusive propositions. Judge Fletcher had four children and founded the Federal Judges Association, and, according to Judge Williams, she was as comfortable with the cleaning staff as she was with justices of the Supreme Court. Judge Williams learned practical life lessons about balance and success through these deep, long-term mentoring relationships.

Judge Williams found that she, like her mentors, had strength of will that was critical to stay the course and achieve her goals. Judge Williams reflects of Judge Motley, and herself, "Many people discouraged her, but it never deterred her. In fact, the effect was the exact opposite. I too learned that I would not be put down, and that my race or sex would not determine my course in life. I found that the detractors that cropped up only spurred me on to succeed."

Judge Williams reveals that she didn't always know she wanted to be a judge. During her tenure at the US Attorney's Office, there were only a handful of African American judges on the court and, before her appointment, only eight African American women had been appointed to the federal bench. Not only were mentors critical to Judge Williams's path, but she shares that a team of supporters was also key. Someone recommended Judge Williams for a seat and, she reflects, that was the first time sitting on the bench had entered her mind. Even then she did not take the notion seriously until she was asked to apply by the US Attorney.

Judge Williams shares that her key to success is communication. In addition to having a long-standing trial practice, prior to practicing law she worked as a teacher. Even now she continues to teach at Northwestern Law School. As a teacher, she sees the importance of being able to communicate with people and present ideas in a way they can be understood. Judge Williams advises, "Communicate! Break it down. Be persuasive. Provide counsel. Those skills work." And don't let your youth or inexperience stop you, she continues.

Judge Williams led organizations from a young age, and even the newest and youngest among us can do it, she encourages. Hopefully, you will have some of the support systems that Judge Williams had. She relates how her family created an incredible sense of support:

*My parents believed in me, and said, "You can do anything if you work hard and never let anyone turn you back." My parents were tremendous role models and taught me that with great rewards come great responsibilities. I had the privilege of going to college at the same time as my dad, who had saved his money to go back, and he had a deep and abiding faith in my ability. Even from a young age, because of my support system, someone telling me no was a dare. That was a laying down of the gauntlet, and I had to prove them wrong.*

Judge Williams urges women to find the cause or issue that they care most about and make a difference. Work within existing organizations to effect change. Judge Williams closed with this charge:

*One person can make a difference. You can impact the world. Even greater, if you are joined with others, you can REALLY make a difference. If you have a great idea, get others to join with you. Have the vision, understand people, and know that the opportunities given to you are real blessings. **If the choice is should you lead, then you must lead because you have a responsibility to give back.** You do not need a black robe to lead. You can do it as a young lawyer or a seasoned lawyer or wherever you are. Lead.*

Talk about someone laying down the gauntlet. Now it is up to us to follow through on the charge.

**Judge Angela M. Bradstreet**
San Francisco Superior Court
*Be true to yourself.*

Authenticity is not only Judge Angela M. Bradstreet's life motto, born out of life experience, it is also the first thing you notice when interacting with her. She kicks off conversations with transparency that builds an immediate connection. Judge Bradstreet has maintained that authentic sense of self throughout various phases of her successful career in law. Before Governor Arnold Schwarzenegger appointed Judge Bradstreet, she served as the state labor commissioner, the managing partner of a private law firm, and as president of numerous associations and organizations. Judge Bradstreet shared that early times of adversity were character-building: "They gave me inner strength and enabled me to be true to myself, even in my career." Part of that authenticity is reflected in Judge Bradstreet's role as the president and leader of multiple bar associations and community groups. Judge Bradstreet explains that it all stems from the importance of giving back to your community.

> *Part of a meaningful legal career is giving back to our community. The most effective leaders look beyond the boundaries of their workplaces to reach out to the community to make a difference, whether it is through bar association work, volunteering in a nonprofit, or advancing equality for minorities, women, and gays and lesbians in the legal profession. Whatever your passion is in this regard, follow it!*

Judge Bradstreet recounted that her commitment to authenticity presented new challenges during her stint as managing partner of a law firm. She noted the importance of knowing who she was and remaining true to that: "You have to try not to emulate others, but develop your own style and your own sense of self." She emphasized that both judges and juries can quickly suss out when lawyers are not authentic, and they are less likely to succeed in the courtroom, and in life.

In addition to authenticity, Judge Bradstreet highlights several skills she has witnessed that intrinsically create dynamic women leaders. First and foremost, Judge Bradstreet emphasizes, are the natural collaborative interpersonal skills women possess. Not only is it important to use those skills to achieve your goals, Judge Bradstreet says, but we must recognize that we possess unique skills that qualify us for leadership. But Judge Bradstreet has found that the gender differences can present obstacles as well. First, women must not be reticent to ask for what they want. Second, women have to stop personalizing every career setback. Judge Bradstreet recalls women lawyers who have come to her to beat themselves up about a lost motion or trial, and they have personalized the loss instead of appreciating that certain circumstances were beyond their control. Judge Bradstreet continues, "Men don't do that, and women shouldn't. In my two terms as managing partner, I learned not to personalize things. I also learned that perception can be more important than reality. Go ahead and allow yourself to feel emotion about a circumstance, but do not portray that emotion. I went to great lengths to show I was not taking things at work personally."

Another critical trait to develop as a leader is engendering trust, according to Judge Bradstreet. She advises that your word must be your bond: "Build trust. Build it with everyone. Build it with the judge and the jury. Build it with your peers and your colleagues. That, in turn, builds your reputation and enhances your ability to lead others. Reputation is everything. Consider that in all you do."

Judge Bradstreet gives the insightful analogy between a skilled leader and a skilled brief writer. Of the brief-writing lawyer, she says, "You have to earn trust. Even in what you write. I read papers and briefs and the attorneys must relay information and analysis in the brief that is true. Acknowledge the weaknesses up front. Then distinguish them. Be well prepared. Be flexible. And have a backup position." This is exactly what a leader must do, Judge Bradstreet continues.

*A leader emphasizes their skill set, identifies any weaknesses, but frames them or distinguishes them so that their leadership is still supported by the team or followers. Be prepared with your plan but understand that things change, and be flexible enough to change with the circumstances and obstacles that require developing alternative paths. And have a fallback plan. Know that sometimes the path changes and that learning experience will end up being more valuable to your leadership growth and journey than your initial plan could have been. Sometimes it is the route we couldn't imagine that leads to the greatest opportunities, and a true leader acknowledges those opportunities.*

Another key leadership skill to develop is superior people skills. Judge Bradstreet reminds us that communication with others makes all the difference in your career: "If someone doesn't like you or want to be around you, that can create a bad reputation. Be courteous and respectful to everyone. People that like you and respect you will help you succeed. And remember, laugh at yourself. Not at others, but you have to have a sense of humor about your life. Keep everything in perspective."

In closing, one issue on which Judge Bradstreet is an activist is helping women battle internal glass ceilings:

*We as women create our own glass ceilings because of fear or insecurity or apprehension over change. We trap ourselves. We create boundaries that don't exist. We hold on to an untrue belief that we cannot do something or achieve a certain goal. Self-doubt is pervasive. Women must recognize this to overcome it. But if we are going to lead effectively, we have to smash those internal glass ceilings, whatever the reason for their existence.*

Judge Bradstreet has done just that. Shattered her internal, and external, glass ceilings to lead and succeed. As a result, she holds a gavel and wears a robe and inspires us all to shatter our own glass ceilings.

**Justice Fernande R.V. Duffly**
Massachusetts Supreme Judicial Court
*Think big!*

Justice Fernande R.V. Duffly has a remarkable American story. A story of what drives her. A story that inspires those who have had the opportunity to hear her share it. Justice Duffly was born in Indonesia to a Chinese mother and a Dutch father and came to America at the age of six speaking no English. Like so many immigrants, they left family, a home, and a job, looking for better opportunities; they took risks and initially had to rely on the help of others for their basic needs. Through hard work they achieved modest success, and with the support of her parents, Justice Duffly made her way to Harvard Law School in the 1970s, when there were few women attending, and even fewer minorities. After stints as a partner of a venerable Boston law firm and other judicial positions, she ascended to her current position on the Massachusetts Supreme Judicial Court in 2011, but not before she had made several unsuccessful applications for earlier openings on that court.

Justice Duffly says there is a larger purpose in sharing her story. It is a story of overcoming. It is a story that she hopes will urge people to *do* something to make a difference. Provide pro bono representation. Participate in an organization or a project that advances a cause—whatever the cause is. One of the causes she has pursued throughout her career is born from her personal story: advancing women and minorities in ways that will lead to a diverse judiciary and legal profession and to equal access to justice.

Justice Duffly's repeated exhortation to women is to have a mission or a goal, and enlist others to help you reach it. Dream big!

*You must believe in your goal and convey it in a way that inspires others to believe it, too. You can't just order people to help you achieve your dreams and goals; you have to make them believe in it and want to do it because they truly believe in its importance. In addition, you must provide specific steps to reach the goal. Start small—it's one baby step after another that leads to*

*the ultimate result. Although having a goal facilitates effective decision mak-*
*ing—you can know what choices to make because you do it all with an eye*
*toward that goal—you also need to be flexible and understand that you have*
*to love the journey and the path that takes you there. Love the path because*
*you may not get to the place you originally set out to reach, but if you enjoy*
*the journey you will still find yourself in a fulfilling place.*

Justice Duffly also stresses the importance of building a consortium:

*As you set out on your journey to achieve your goals, bring like-minded people*
*together. My approach has always been to bring people together to achieve a com-*
*mon goal. That team will help to accomplish far more than you could ever accom-*
*plish on your own.*

While studying law at Harvard, Justice Duffly noticed the lack of women and
minorities and wondered, "How do we change this?" The assistant dean, who
was also the director of admissions, said the issue was the lack of diversity in
the application pool. So Justice Duffly, then "Nan," asked for funding so that she
and a team of friends could travel to "feeder" schools to meet with women and
minority groups and encourage them to apply to Harvard. They then created a
group of women phone-mentors for candidates who received offers to attend.
Justice Duffly and her team believed they could change the entire profession by
diversifying the pool of law students who would one day take on leadership roles
in law, government, and business, and she developed specific steps to effectuate
the change they wished to see.

*More women and minorities did apply, and were accepted. But years later,*
*I was dismayed to realize that the numbers did not take care of themselves,*
*that more had to be done to achieve the goal of a diverse legal profession. So,*
*we're still working at it.*

Justice Duffly has consistently taken this team-building approach to continuing this work. She led the National Association of Women Judges, which seeks to
"promote the judicial role of protecting the rights of individuals under the rule
of law through strong, committed, diverse judicial leadership." Through organizations such as NAWJ, the ABA, and women and minority bar associations, she
has focused on what women practitioners, including women of color, need to
advance and how we can help each other to "really amplify the voice of women

across the board." Confronting obstacles along the way, she says, it is easier to press on with the support of "a large community of people who want to achieve the same goals."

In her advice to women starting out, Justice Duffly encourages curiosity. "Listen to women, find out how they did what they did, and then ask questions as to how you might achieve your goals," she says. Being an effective leader also requires you to listen, she says, finding common ground in differing perspectives and allowing everyone the dignity of having a chance to articulate their viewpoint. In the courtroom or in the office, "you want people to feel they had a chance to speak, that you acknowledge the value of what is said and incorporate different perspectives into the big picture—that lends itself to a positive experience," she says.

In the long line of leaders encouraging us to stick with it, Justice Duffly reminds us that achieving our goals could take time, and we won't get there if we aren't good at what we do. She recommends that we acknowledge what we want to do and let our team members know it. In order to ultimately reach the pinnacle, you need a vast supporting network, and those folks must have connections they are willing to share. Justice Duffly gives this practical advice:

> *Start with the people who know you and think you walk on water. Once they see your goals and ambitions, then they can reach out to those they know, set up meetings, vouch for you. You can then begin building an expanded network with those people. In these conversations with an ever-growing network, you should seek advice instead of just support (and never call people up cold). This is a two-way street—give people the opportunity to be excited about your goal and then develop the relationship. But be willing to promote yourself. You have to believe in yourself, the product, and then sell the product. Explain to your team and supporters, "Here's why I can do this and what I've learned about what I could do and why I'd like to do it."*

Justice Duffly credits her father for her insight into selling oneself and one's goals. He could not speak English when he came to America, but he eventually got a job selling life insurance because he genuinely believed that it was important for even poor people to have it in order to protect their families. Although the language barriers should have made him a poor salesman, he transcended such barriers because he believed in what he was doing. Find pockets of time to look for leadership opportunities where you can develop your skills while pursuing a cause about which you are passionate, Justice Duffly urges. Do something significant. "If you're not going to do it *and love it*, you won't excel at the job," she says. "So lead in an arena you love."

What an impressive reminder that authenticity can transcend barriers and obstacles to achieving the goals we are passionate about.

**Judge Vanessa Ruiz**
DC Court of Appeals
*View your differences as assets.*

From her private practice with international clients, to being one of the few women to argue a case in front of the Supreme Court in the early 1980s when she was a young lawyer, to being the first (and only) Hispanic to serve as attorney general for the District of Columbia, to her 1994 appointment by President Clinton as the first (and only) Hispanic to the highest court of the District of Columbia, Judge Vanessa Ruiz has had an impressive and remarkable run as a leading woman in the law. Yet you would never know she has achieved these distinctions because of the immediate warmth she offers to those she meets and the willingness with which she shares her experiences and advice. She laughingly begins her list of leadership necessities with, "You have to have followers! But in truth, you do have to have those willing to congregate around you so you can lead."

Judge Ruiz sees the value in much of the "corporate speak" around team building and finds that skill critical to the leadership path. A true leader, Judge Ruiz offers, actively engages in team building and a willingness to bring people along with them. You must be inspirational and teach through example.

Judge Ruiz highlights the misconception that true leaders are "way up there above everyone else." That is not the reflection of a true leader, she cautions. It is just someone striking out on her own path, not necessarily being a leader. You must first be a part of the group, the team, the company, the organization, in order to know how to lead it.

One of the most critical leadership skills to possess is an ability to just be who you are, Judge Ruiz shares: "You will never be as good at being someone else, but you are the best at being you. You can only be a leader, or be good at anything, if you are true to what you believe and you go for it. You must constantly be pushing in that direction." Judge Ruiz reveals that she learned that lesson when she began her career in the 1970s and was one of only a few women and the only Hispanic at her firm. The prevailing notion of the period was that she had to assimilate in order to become a leader and a success. Judge Ruiz continues:

*The thought was that women had to do things the way guys did it, even down to how you dressed. This idea was exacerbated in my own mind by the fact that I was starting out and was not yet sure of my skills and what I could do—you just keep your head down and do whatever needs to get done. At some point, it just hit me that I could not—would not—live my life that way. I would practice law in a way that reflected what I cared about and where I came from. Instead of being like other lawyers, I would be a Hispanic female lawyer and I would approach my work from that perspective. Even the fact that my first language was Spanish taught me to communicate well with international clients; I knew to slow down and repeat things in different ways because I knew that would be helpful to someone whose first language was not English. I had a different perspective because of my different cultural background. View your differences as assets. Those are the things you uniquely bring to the table.*

Community is critical to a leader, Judge Ruiz counsels. You have to be with people, be nurtured by people, and have exchanges with people. That helps you gain direction. You should seek a mentor and be a mentor. Judge Ruiz shares about one of her own mentoring relationships, with Justice Ruth Bader Ginsburg. Originally, the justice had inspired her confidence when Judge Ruiz had a pro bono case five years out of law school that she argued before the Supreme Court and won. So years later, when Judge Ruiz was considering applying for a judgeship, she called Justice Ginsburg for advice, and Justice Ginsburg welcomed her inquiries with warmth and walked her through the process to help her understand what to expect. Then Justice Ginsburg advised her to do it, "just do it!" That is the advice Judge Ruiz has taken to heart and most often gives: **Just do it!** That relationship also taught her that not only can you learn from those who go before you, but you should help others along the way as people have generously helped you. Those relationships in which you can be the mentor build your confidence by reminding you of what you have learned and accomplished in addition to helping others out.

Judge Ruiz says that she still can learn by observing other people, but invariably the people who are most influential and leave the most significant impression are those who are genuine and authentic and direct. She admires those who are comfortable being themselves, with energy and conviction. To do this, to live authentically, you have to be strong, Judge Ruiz reflects: *Know who you are. Be willing to be criticized. Be courageous.* She has found this even more acutely as a judge. A good judge is competent and independent-minded, and knows the law, but a great judge must also be courageous, which is an often overlooked, but critical, trait, according to Judge Ruiz. If you are truly grounded in who you are, you will be able to stand up during times of criticism. In this respect, a leader must be willing to stand alone and take the heat.

With regard to mapping out a strategy and laying out a ten-point plan, Judge Ruiz says she never had one. Her development and growth were "organic." Judge Ruiz says of her path:

> *It was born out of recognizing opportunity when it presented itself, or even better, making an opportunity and then going for it! The outcome may not be what you expect, or even when you expect it, but you can't be afraid of change or the results. Do not be afraid of living your life.*

On failure, Judge Ruiz half-jokingly advises, "First you have a good cry, and curse, and then you go for a run. But then you pick yourself up! You could go back and rethink it all, but really it's not that valuable to hit replay repeatedly." And with regard to criticism, Judge Ruiz warns that you cannot guard against it:

> *The best line of defense is developing relationships and talking with the people you are likely to come into conflict with so that the criticism is on the merits instead of being personal. That also gives you an avenue to change minds. Simple statements are the most impactful in discussions since there's so much noise swirling about. Regardless, once you build up trust and respect, even when people's views remain at odds, you can still engage in substantive discussions and live to engage another day if you've made investments in personal relationships over time.*

Judge Ruiz emphasizes that relationship building is a critical skill to have as a leader. It is not simply about "who you know" but taking the time and making the investment in others that help you on the journey. Then, once they know you, it makes what you do and say carry more weight. Act with integrity, Judge Ruiz underscores, because people respect that. And you will respect yourself.

Judge Ruiz finds truth and inspiration in a poem titled *Traveller,* by Spanish poet Antonio Machado, translated below.

*Traveller, your footprints*
*Are the path and nothing more;*
*Traveller, there is no path,*
*The path is made by walking.*
*By walking the path is made.*

Judge Ruiz closes, "That's the point. You have to make your own path. What you have done propels you to where you are going. My charge: No fear. Have courage. Do it!"

If that charge doesn't inspire us all to act, then nothing will. Start walking, traveller.

# 7

# Total Leadership Makeover

## Transforming Real-Life Lawyers

*The challenges of change are always hard. It is important that we begin to unpack those challenges that confront this nation and realize that we each have a role that requires us to change and become more responsible for shaping our own future.*

—Hillary Rodham Clinton, former First Lady, senator, and secretary of state

*A mistake is simply another way of doing things.*

—Katharine Graham, publisher, chairman of the board, *The Washington Post*

*How wonderful it is that nobody need wait a single moment before starting to improve the world.*

—Anne Frank

■ ■ ■

Now it's application time.

You know the statistics. You understand better the research on effective leadership. You even have a tool kit of tricks and tips from a variety of leading books and articles on leading effectively.

Plus, you have heard from the best and the brightest. Women leading in today's legal marketplaces—corporate, private practice, government, and nonprofit. You have read the words of wisdom from women leading in America's judicial system.

At the end of the day, though, it's all just words on the page. Until you put it into action.

You can best apply these nuggets to your own life by seeing it applied in the lives of others. Prepare to watch five women lawyers' leadership transformations in the following pages. Using the lessons learned and the techniques outlined throughout this book, these five women of different ages, stages, and practices will undergo a total leadership makeover. Each of you is at a different stage of your legal career. Some of you have more leadership ambition than others. For some, much of what was outlined in chapter 4 was old news, while others heard it for the first time. Regardless of where you are at in your own journey, the purpose of sharing these makeovers is to inspire you and encourage you to apply one of the *To-Do List* action items in your own life. Hopefully, seeing these lawyers' career confusion turn into clarity and their limbo turn into leadership will energize you to take affirmative steps in your career to "be the change you wish to see."

## AMY, PRACTICING FIVE YEARS, WANTS TO MAKE PARTNER AND RUN FOR JUDGE

Amy is used to things coming easily to her. She grew up in the town where she was born, had the same friends, made straight As, and served as class president. She took college by storm and easily gained admission to law school at her undergrad alma mater. She spent the summer at a large firm after her second year and received an offer to return after graduation. Amy finished law school and moved into an apartment near work so she could work long hours and prove herself. Turns out, law firm life is harder than anything Amy has ever tackled before. She has lost touch with many of her friends and connections because she works late nights. She feels disconnected from the world at large and isn't taking the time anymore to give back to her community. She works for an older partner who has some interesting notions about the practice of law. His clients are his, and she has not had the chance to meet and build relationships with clients. Her firm does not have a strong associate program, and there has been a real lack of integration of Amy into the larger firm activities and committees. Amy feels like a number and doesn't have a mentor or friend at her firm to connect her to the larger firm culture. Her goal is to become an equity partner in the next couple years, but she has no idea what she needs to do to stand out as a lawyer with leadership potential that the firm should value. She now questions if she should stay at this firm, but with the market being as dismal as it is, and her reviews being solid, she would like to first see if she can turn the ship around where she is before she sets out to distinguish herself as a junior litigator in the larger legal market. Additionally, she has always wanted to become a judge and, in her state, judges are elected. She loves elections, ran for various student body offices, and volunteered on others' political campaigns, but she feels that she must make partner before she considers politics.

### WHAT SHOULD AMY DO?

We heard from women legal leaders and our women judges for whom mentors played a critical role in their leadership potential development. One glaring absence in Amy's career is a mentor relationship. For whatever reason, Amy has not sought out, or found, women with positions of influence or respect within her firm. This could be a female partner, counsel, or a well-respected senior associate. Even if the woman at the firm is not her primary and best mentor relationship, she should seek out someone at the firm to help her really translate the firm culture, how to get ahead, how to land plum assignments, what it takes to make partner, and other intangibles that she wouldn't even know to consider. Additionally, while that insider relationship is critical, particularly if she wants to turn things around at her firm, Amy could also seek mentors and "sponsors" outside of her firm through a women's bar association, a specialty bar group, or even an industry group in the area of law she practices (a women's energy group if she handles litigation for large energy companies, for example). A sponsor would help promote Amy and identify opportunities for her that she, with her limited experience, would not be able to find on her own.

In addition, Amy needs to speak up. It appears as though Amy has taken the situation at face value without believing she has control over the situation. She needs to chart her own course by speaking out, respectfully and mindfully, but clearly. She can first approach the primary partner in charge of her development and project assignments. Amy has received positive reviews even if her working relationship hasn't been ideal. She should approach the partner and ask for more direct client interaction and to attend client meetings with him even if the time has to be written off for a few lunches. The face-to-face interaction is far more valuable than a few lost hours. She should consider these types of "investment" opportunities. Additionally, if there are other partners working on projects she finds particularly interesting, she should let them know she would like to pitch in when the newest matter with that specialty comes in. She must also develop relationships with the members of the management or executive committees so that the people who ultimately will be voting on her promotion will know who she is and what she stands for.

Finally, she should not accept at face value that there is only one road to becoming a judge. It certainly doesn't follow that you have to be a partner of a large firm. What level of court does she want to serve on? What are her ambitions after election? She should begin thinking long term and then as a part of her effort to develop sponsor relationships, find those that have run for judge at different ages and stages of their careers. Also, if she truly has this vision, she must speak out about it and communicate her wishes to those people already on her "team." She has been so focused on the immediate that she has lost sight of the long term and the relationships and activities she must undertake to develop grassroots support. Could she run for the board of her neighborhood association as practice? For the school board? Are there local activities where she can better understand campaigns and politics, and develop local supporters for a judicial campaign later on?

### AMY'S TO-DO LIST:

1. Identify two potential women mentors/sponsors inside the firm and two women outside the firm that she could reach out to and ask to visit with about her career goals and ambitions. Have a clear conversation with her partner regarding client interaction. Identify other partners and committees she can get involved with and develop relationships with at the firm.

2. Understand what the firm's policy is on the advancement of women. Investigate her opportunities within the firm over the next year, and if it turns out it is not the best fit for her professional ambitions, begin to identify other job opportunities regardless of the risk that brings. More risky is staying unfulfilled and disconnected at her current firm indefinitely.

3. Begin identifying independent political goals and action items. Develop a list of ways to connect to the local community. Run for a small office that begins to build a community of grassroots supporters. Seek out younger judges to see what they did that worked for their campaigns. Don't let this dream fall to the bottom where it is neglected because it is less immediate.

## ALICE, PRACTICING TEN YEARS, WANTS TO MOVE FROM GOVERNMENT TO CORPORATE

Alice is stuck. She's an effective lawyer with an impressive American dream story. In fact, Alice is an expert in compliance legal issues and has argued successfully before every kind of court, including scoring impressive victories in federal appellate courts. However, she has not been happy at her job for a long time. She has a laundry list of organizations she has led effectively, but it has been a few years and she cannot seem to make a leadership mark in her day-to-day practice. Also, she knows she will likely never have the potential to be a standout leader where she works currently. Alice has spent over a year trying to transition out of her mundane government job to a corporate counsel position where there will be both more stimulating work and an opportunity for her to lead and succeed in her career. She has even been on a number of finalist lists, but something always falls through, much to her dismay. The time she did receive an offer at a new company, she realized the position ultimately would not offer her the work and opportunities to lead and the stimulation that she desires. Because of her frustration, and an ever-increasing negative narrative that is running on a loop through her head, Alice has started seeking any job change instead of strategically focusing on what she wants to do and what would allow her the most opportunity.

### WHAT SHOULD ALICE DO?

Our panel of experts thought about what tools would be most effective for Alice to utilize. The first critical tool is building, and expanding, on her relationships. *Networking* is an overused word, but the reality is that Alice is not connecting to the people that make the decisions or the people who have the ear of the decision makers. After Alice's last leadership positions, she did not identify the avenues to stay connected to those with corporate positions and connections. Therefore, when a new opportunity crops up, Alice will not have a close enough relationship to anyone to ask for assistance opening that door or connecting her to a team willing to support her in achieving her goals.

Next, Alice has fallen prey to one of the oldest and most pervasive myths that impede women from climbing the leadership ladder: *Work hard and you'll get noticed.* Alice is actually an incredibly successful lawyer. She has served on executive committees of large nonprofit organizations, she has won complex compliance cases because of her advocacy, she leads and volunteers with much success, and she is a self-made woman who came from challenging socio-economic circumstances and a family with no lawyers or post-graduate education in their ranks. She did not attend a top-tier law school, but her work has been met with great feedback from clients and supervisors alike. She does struggle against the obstacle of having worked in the government sector for an extended period, which can create the misconception that she is content to stay in the government ranks or that she would be unable to make the transition to the corporate mind-set.

So Alice's hard work is all for naught in the job market unless she really sells herself. From the outset, her résumé and letters/e-mails/telephone calls must communicate confidence, showcase successes, and laud leadership. Alice is a go-getter and that attitude must come through every aspect of what she does in the interview process. She needs to think of this process as branding. Many women shrink from the idea of "branding" themselves for fear that it might read as self-promotional, but each person IS their own brand. (Plus, there is nothing wrong with self-promoting when you seek to take the next big step!) Your brand is the biggest selling point you have. A brand is simply what makes each practitioner unique. Alice's "brand" makes Alice unique. Alice must sell herself as a self-starting, self-made woman who succeeds at everything she tackles and takes risks to ensure the biggest possible successes. Rebranding herself will not only help Alice conquer the job market, but it will also help Alice reframe the increasing negative story line in her own head into a story line of achievement and empowerment. That hits on two key leadership skills that are a must on any effective leader's list: optimism and self-promotion.

### ALICE'S TO-DO LIST:

1. Make a list of the top ten companies in the region she lives in where she would like to work. Make a list of her connections in that region. Using all the social media she already has at her fingertips, such as LinkedIn and Facebook, she can reach out to connections or add connections she previously failed to capture. Rank them to see who is most likely to be in a position to help her or know someone who could. Call the top twenty (or more). Take the friends to coffee or lunch. Make a timeline.

2. Rebrand. Have friends look over and critique her résumé and cover letter. Invite five friends out for a glass of wine to talk through possible interview discussion points and sample questions.

3. As a part of that effort, develop a list of her successes as well as her goals. She must know her résumé and brand. Make sure she has an elevator speech at the ready for encounters with potential employers or sponsors and supporters. Begin participating in in-person networking events where she can practice delivering her message. To achieve the next steps, she must communicate her message to a wider audience.

## AUDREY, PRACTICING FIFTEEN YEARS, NOT SURE WHAT'S NEXT

Audrey is at a crossroads. While she never dreamed of becoming a lawyer, she actually does love her career. She married after practicing nearly ten years, and not long after that she had children. She's worked in private practice and excelled, but now with young children at home she finds it is harder to juggle the unpredictability of her young partnership. She wants to continue working, but she's not sure what her options are. Should she look for a smaller firm that has, possibly, more balance embedded in its model? Should she consider moving to an in-house legal department as many of her working-mother friends have? Should she do something more noble with her career like nonprofit or government work? Or maybe she can make her current job work. She doesn't know what will work, yet she is not willing to bail out on the profession. Plus, her family relies on having two incomes. Over the course of her career, even her life, she has led effectively. From student bodies to charities and associations, she truly enjoys having a voice and creating change. She has a vast network of connections and enjoys working collaboratively to problem-solve. Yet, for the first time, she has no idea what that looks like for her career. She has taken calls from recruiters and talked to some potential new employers, but is uncertain about whether she's willing to make a change and is nervous about having to re-prove herself after all this time. And while she is ambitious, she feels that for a season, her ambition needs to take a back seat as she figures out how to be a mom and a wife and a daughter to aging parents. The juggling feels impractical in her current environment.

### WHAT SHOULD AUDREY DO?

There are two key elements our experts noted immediately that are lacking from Audrey's desire to do something different: vision and moving forward under her own initiative. Experts and the research both support the proposition that the path to career success and leadership does not have to be linear, and oftentimes women must deviate from their set course because of relationships, health, children, and aging parents. The fact that a career looks a lot more like the waves of an ocean than a stepladder does not preclude satisfaction and success. In fact, more often than not, that is how many leading women found their ultimate career satisfaction. Furthermore, Audrey has decided she does not want to leave the workforce but rather just wants to shift gears for this season. That honesty regarding her current circumstances is wise. However, Audrey cannot make an informed decision about what is right for this season, nor can she enlist support-ers to help her transition, unless she develops goals and a new vision.

Audrey's vision cannot be one of her career or leadership opportunities in a vacuum—it has to be a vision with a holistic understanding of her life's demands now and changes to those demands in the future. Women do not have to adopt a traditional timeline for career progression down a straight track. The reality is, detours occur, and those lead to passions, opportunities, and new paths.

First, Audrey needs to determine how much she is available to work. Is it just that 10 p.m. calls and unexpected weekends on duty make her current job impractical? Or is it the entire system and setup at her current place of employ-ment? If the former, then she can negotiate better arrangements with the execu-tive team to ensure her current workplace remains workable in her new life circumstance. However, if the demands of the monthly billable-hour require-ment and constant need to generate new clients are proving all-consuming, then looking at alternative work environments may be necessary. What type of lead-ership opportunities and promotions would she like to have available? What type of flexible work accommodations does she need? What is the prospective company's or firm's required talent-development approach? The problem is, without Audrey answering these questions first, she can't know when and how to step out and act.

Second, Audrey needs to take action and make decisions. She has visited with recruiters and lawyers she knows and has somewhat haphazardly been mak-ing connections for new jobs she hears about, but she has no strategy and still doesn't know what she wants going in. Once she has set out her vision, she needs to act. Audrey will have to set achievable targets with calendar appointments and deadlines every week, otherwise her action items will get lost in the shuffle of family activities and work demands. The carve-outs on her calendar for affirma-tive action should be treated as would any other client appointment. While step-ping into the unknown is always unnerving, being in charge of her own career path and leadership possibilities is required and risk is inevitable.

Finally, Audrey is well-connected. She should sit down with some of her best supporters, mentors, sponsors, and cheerleaders, those outside of her current place of employment, and get an objective perspective about what opportuni-ties might exist that she has not recognized, as well as understand from working mothers that have gone before her what worked and what did not work so she can better map out her plan of attack.

## AUDREY'S TO-DO LIST:

1. Find her vision. While Audrey may not traditionally have had goals or a vision for her career, it's time she developed them. Not only will it guide her during this critical crossroad period, it will significantly improve her leadership skills. People will not follow a leader without a vision. If she cannot develop a vision for her own life, then she will not be able to lead as a visionary in her current or new organization. Talk to her husband and her parents and her friends and her mentors. Get buy-in from the key people in her life, but ultimately Audrey will have to live with the road she chooses.

2. Take matters into her own hands. Once she has laid out what she wants in the short term and long term for her career, then she must take affirmative steps to make that happen. If it's time to move from her current firm, then she needs to collect the names of a few of the best recruiters in her area of practice. She should mine her network to find out what opportunities exist and which ones best match up to her priorities. She shouldn't shortchange her assessment of the long-term options even though it is her short-term situation that is driving the change. She must calendar time every week to complete these action items.

3. Connect. Oftentimes when major life changes happen, like caring for young children or aging parents, women become disconnected from their friends and supporters. Time constraints do exist, but Audrey must prioritize maintaining relationships, which not only will help her in the future as she seeks to develop her leadership potential, but even more importantly will give her an outlet to connect and decompress and be encouraged.

## ANNE, PRACTICING NINETEEN YEARS, WANTS CORPORATE EXECUTIVE AND BOARD POSITIONS

Anne is hardworking and resilient. Her family was in the military and so was she, briefly. When she left the military, she finished her undergraduate degree, worked for a couple years, and then went back to law school. She found success often. She worked in private practice and the government before being appointed the assistant general counsel for a Fortune 500 company. She thrived in the corporate environment because she had an understanding of business as well as the law. She has faced a number of gender stereotypes in her workplace but either did not recognize them or had no idea how to combat them. At times, she tried to model some of the "successful" characteristics of her male counterparts that created their promotion opportunities, but to no avail. She served in the military decades ago, so she knows how to act like a man if she needs to. Anne is both tough and ambitious, but for the first time her ambition seems to have run into a brick wall. In order to continue up the corporate leadership, and eventually make herself valuable enough to sit on corporate boards and serve in a major corporate executive circle, she has to do something differently.

### WHAT SHOULD ANNE DO?

Anne clearly has a vision and is working in earnest to achieve it—she wants to climb the corporate ladder, eventually moving beyond the law department, and she wants to show she can be a value added to corporate boards. She believes she is uniquely qualified because of her diversified background, yet she's not seeing any progress. Our panel of experts said the first obstacle Anne must overcome is her inclination to emulate others instead of acting in a way that reflects who she is. It's unclear whether she knows who she is, but constantly remodeling herself to try to copy techniques that worked for others, mainly men, will not work if she wants to succeed on a grander scale. Just as one of the authors we cited noted, you cannot be successful if you are not authentic, and you cannot be authentic by trying to be like someone else. Anne needs to make a list of her strengths and the reasons she believes she is uniquely qualified to achieve these next leadership goals. She needs to believe them and communicate them.

Anne does not share whether she has a network of supporters and sponsors, but to take a step in the next leadership rung, both will be critical components for success. She should chart the people she has in her network, the strategic people, and identify whether they will help connect her, promote her, inform her about the politics of taking the next step, educate her about the realities of the new positions, or otherwise play a key role in her achieving the next steps. Once she's made that list or chart, then she can identify where there are gaps and fill them in with new relationships she should begin to build. Additionally, once she reaches out to both new and existing strategic partners in her network, she should reciprocate. Networking is a two-way street. Is there something that her partners need from her? Support or encouragement or knowledge? All the old adages support that—be a friend to have a friend, do unto others, and so on.

Additionally, many of her counterparts moving from law to business have an MBA. One expert suggests that she go to night or weekend classes to obtain an MBA to show the corporation, her current one or the next one, that she is serious about knowing business and being more than just a lawyer in the company. She has shown she has a knack for business, but oftentimes credentials do matter and she may need to take one more leap to get the job she wants. Plus, MBA classes may educate her even more about what to look for in high-functioning corporate boards, and she can understand where value can most significantly be added.

## ANNE'S TO-DO LIST:

1. Make a list of her strengths and weaknesses. Understand where she adds value to her company and beyond the law department. Stop trying to emulate what works for the men receiving promotions in her field and instead know who she is and be the best version of herself. That authenticity will make her a leader people can trust.
2. Develop a strategic networking spreadsheet. List who supports critical components of her next steps. Reach out to them. Communicate her vision to them to enlist their support. Find out how she can reciprocate. And fill in gaps in her network with new relationships. Think strategically.
3. Consider continuing education. Possibly an MBA program. If she wants to move into a business arena from law eventually, then having the pedigree may help.

## ANGELA, PRACTICING TWENTY-FOUR YEARS, WANTS A SECOND CAREER AS A SOLO PRACTITIONER

Angela married before law school and had her first child while a 2L. She found out she was pregnant with her second while studying for the bar. Nothing shook out like she expected. She worked hard but never felt like she had a choice about where she worked. Since her divorce, every decision she has made felt "necessary." She has held a number of jobs, and sometimes even took a second job when her legal job wasn't paying the bills like she had expected. Her kids have finally left the house, and she feels like she can actually do what she has always wanted to do. She wants to become a leading voice in elder care law. She watched with great sadness some of the injustice her aging parents suffered, but she felt like she did not have the voice to speak out and effect change because of her limited knowledge base and her limited connections within the legal community. Her two decades of experience were largely devoid of relationships, either personal or professional networking, because so often she operated on survival mode. She believes she is ready to take a risk and learn a new area and set out on her own, but after years of quashing her gut instinct, she has no idea where to start. Plus, she holds tightly to the myth that she has to do it all, all by herself, and since her savings are not substantial, she does have to earn a living at whatever she decides to do.

### WHAT SHOULD ANGELA DO?

First, our panel of experts applauds Angela for pushing reset and creating a new vision for herself. So often people fall into the trap of believing that they cannot create a new vision for their career, or that they have missed out on the leadership opportunity, because their current job is the only thing they've ever done and they've done it for some time. One of the pieces of wisdom from the women interviewed is that women have to get over the idea that a career is linear. Women have all sorts of obstacles in their careers, and as long as critical leadership years fall at the same time as child-rearing years and aging-parent care years, there will always be growth and setbacks in a woman's career. Accept that it is part of the process, and re-chart your course when you have newfound freedom from childcare or parent care. Here, Angela is taking on three key successful leadership characteristics in one bite: having a vision, taking risks, and charting her own course. So now what for Angela, since she's taken those initial steps?

As is clear in each of these women's lives, relationships are key. Angela has a different set of relationships she needs, though, to achieve her vision. First, is she clear on what her vision is? Does she want her own practice, or would she consider sharing a practice with another person? That enables her to have backup as well as another knowledge source when a thorny issue arises. If she really wants to make a difference, would she consider running for elected office? A state or federal legislator (or a judge in certain cases)? If she believes that having her own practice is really her ultimate vision, then she has to start building up her knowledge, her resources, and her clients.

There are several kinds of relationships she needs to develop. She needs to have resource relationships with lawyers who can provide support and camaraderie. She should seek out bar associations (local is particularly helpful, but also state and national) for solo and small practitioners as well as for wills and estates lawyers. This will not only plug her into the community in which she wants to serve but give her credibility and relevant CLE. She also needs to begin to build a reputation for practicing and practicing well in the community. There are numerous legal aid organizations, senior centers, and wills clinics where she can cut her teeth. This will not only give her relevant knowledge but also provide a rewarding experience where she can have a voice in seniors' lives that she felt she lacked when her parents were struggling.

Next, she needs to develop mentors and sponsors. In Angela's situation, mentors may actually be more critical than sponsors in the first instance. She needs to talk to other people who have practiced alone, who have shared offices, who have developed a partnership, and other similar options for her. This does not have to be in the area of law she wishes to practice, but rather should address organizational and development goals. Additionally, she also needs to develop friendships and colleagues. She has neglected her own personal well-being and emotional growth because of constant worrying about bills and family. It's time that Angela developed relationships with people that she can laugh with, cry with, and dream with. Particularly given that she will be going through big life changes with these career changes, she will need additional emotional support via relationships.

While relationships are certainly the most important part of Angela's leadership plan, she should also cultivate other leadership characteristics in order to build her brand and business. As she volunteers, she should have contact information and a blurb about her services at the ready in order to develop an impactful business statement that reaches new audiences. She also should be ready to actually take some risk. It is important to know what to do, have a business plan, and determine whether she should be solo or part of a small associated group of lawyers; once she has investigated the options, she must act. It will be scary and she may need to do something at the outset to supplement her income, but it is important that, as she develops her plan and her brand, she actually moves forward and does not get stuck in the research and development phase.

## ANGELA'S TO-DO LIST:

1. Build key relationships. Determine if she has any people currently in her network, but then make a list of areas where her life needs people. Join associations, charities, and legal aid organizations that have similarly situated professionals, but also find something she's passionate about and join that activity, too. She must remain fulfilled professionally and personally for her own well-being.

2. Investigate and then act. Determine whether solo really is the right course or if there is a partner or partners who might ease this transition. Uncover what it takes to start her own practice. Find people who have gone before her to help her understand what she will be taking on.

3. Develop a brand through study, volunteering, and promotion. She must do more wills and estates work to understand the legal side of the business, but she must also undertake a self-assessment to develop her brand and find a memorable way to stand out and market herself. Enlist the support of a new friend or mentor to give her feedback on the ideas.

## CONCLUSION

This summary of leadership techniques did not set out to break new ground but rather to provide lawyers with a fresh perspective on leading effectively. It is a noble profession in which we serve, and it needs dynamic leadership to set an ambitious course. One that combats stereotypes and gender myths. One that values leadership in the private firm, the corporate legal department, the government agency, and all areas in which people holding law degrees serve.

Not everyone wants to be a leader. And rightly so. Nor is being a leader everyone's strong suit. There must be followers. But if you picked this book up, you may have your eye on a leadership role. Whether that is in your legal field or beyond, the role is there for the taking.

1. Be yourself. It sounds as simple as a Mr. Rogers sound bite, but it is the foundation for leadership. Do not conform because of external pressures.
2. Find your inner optimist. That is going to help you bounce back from hardship and build and retain a team and supporters.
3. Take risks. They need to be smart risks, but confidently take a step and stretch beyond your comfort zone.
4. Chart your course. Define what success and leadership look like for you, which can be completely different from everyone else's model, and then go make it happen.
5. Have a vision. Sit down today and figure out what it is you want to achieve. Today and in the future. And allow for that vision to change over time.
6. Build relationships. With everyone. Sponsors, mentors, supporters, and team members.
7. Acknowledge your talent and accomplishments, out loud. You rock. Own that.
8. Speak up. Change will never happen if leaders don't push for it.

In the words of Judge Williams, *One person can make a difference. You can impact the world. Even greater, if you are joined with others, you can REALLY make a difference. Have the vision, understand people, and know that the opportunities given to you are real blessings.* **If the choice is should you lead, then you must lead because you have a responsibility to give back!**

**So let's get leading.**

■ ■ ■

# Appendix A

# Resources

**LEADERSHIP BOOKS REFERENCED AND ADDITIONAL RESOURCES:**

*Break Your Own Rules: How to Change the Patterns of Thinking that Block Women's Paths to Power* by Jill Flynn, Kathryn Heath, and Mary Davis Holt

*Dear Sisters, Dear Daughters: Strategies for Success from Multicultural Women Attorneys*, ABA Commission on Women in the Profession

*The Girl's Guide to Being a Boss (Without Being a Bitch): Valuable Lessons, Smart Suggestions, and True Stories for Succeeding as the Chick-in-Charge (2006)* by Caitlin Friedman and Kimberly Yorio

*How Remarkable Women Lead: The Breakthrough Model for Work and Life* by Joanna Barsh and Susie Cranston

*How Women Lead: The 8 Essential Strategies Successful Women Know* by Sharon Hadary and Laura Henderson

*Lean In: Women, Work, and the Will to Lead* by Sheryl Sandberg

*Secrets of Six-Figure Women* by Barbara Stanny

*Serve to Lead: Your Transformational 21st Century Leadership System* by James M. Strock

*Strengths Based Leadership: Great Leaders, Teams, and Why People Follow* by Tom Rath and Barry Conchie

*Swim with the Dolphins: How Women Can Succeed in Corporate America on Their Own Terms* by Connie Glaser and Barbara Steinberg Smalley

*Through the Labyrinth: The Truth about How Women Become Leaders* by Alice Eagly and Linda Carli

*True North: Discover Your Authentic Leadership* by Bill George and Peter Sims

*Women Don't Ask: Negotiation and the Gender Divide* by Linda Babcock and Sara Laschever

*Womenomics: Write Your Own Rules for Success* by Claire Shipman and Katty Kay

## LEADERSHIP ARTICLES AND WOMEN IN LAW RESEARCH AND REPORTS:

"10 Strategies for Building Leadership Optimism" by Dan McCarthy (April 7, 2009) http://www.greatleadershipbydan.com/2009/04/10-strategies-for-building-leadership.html

"10 Traits of Women Business Leaders" by Matt Symonds (August 8, 2012) http://www.forbes.com/sites/mattsymonds/2012/08/08/10-traits-of-women-business-leaders-its-not-what-you-think/

"10 Traits That Are Essential for Women Leaders" by Lyn Turknett http://www.turknett.com/sectione/documents/WorldWIT7_05TenEssentialTraits.pdf

"Are You Being Strategic about Relationships?" by Neena Newberry http://newberrycoaching.com/2012/are-you-being-strategic-about-relationships/

"Be Somebody—Get Sponsored" by Ilene Lang, Catalyst Blog (August 2010) http://www.catalyst.org/blog/catalyzing/be-somebody%E2%80%94get-sponsored

"Breaking Through the Glass Ceiling—Attaining Equality for Women Lawyers" by Roberta Liebenberg, *U.S. News & World Report* http://bestlawfirms.usnews.com/editorialarticles.aspx?articleid=10

"A Current Glance at Women in the Law (February 2013)" ABA Commission on Women in the Profession http://www.americanbar.org/content/dam/aba/marketing/women/current_glance_statistics_feb2013.pdf

"The Double-Bind Dilemma for Women in Leadership: Damned if You Do, Doomed if You Don't" Catalyst (July 2007) http://www.catalyst.org/knowledge/double-bind-dilemma-women-leadership-damned-if-you-do-doomed-if-you-dont-0

"Four Key Levers to Manage Your Career and Get Results" by Neena Newberry (March 2012) http://newberrycoaching.com/2012/four-key-levers-to-manage-your-career-and-get-results/

"From Visible Invisibility to Visibly Successful: Success Strategies for Law Firms and Women of Color in Law Firms" ABA Commission on Women in the Profession Report http://www.americanbar.org/content/dam/aba/migrated/women/woc/VisiblySuccessful.pdf

"Getting to the Top: Strategies for Breaking through the Glass Ceiling" by Tracey de Morsella http://www.multiculturaladvantage.com/leader/workplace-leadership/Getting-To-The-Top-Strategies-for-Breaking-Through-The-Glass-Ceiling.asp

"Good Intentions, Imperfect Execution? Women Get Fewer of the 'Hot Jobs' Needed to Advance" Catalyst Report (November 2012) http://www.catalyst.org/system/files/Good_Intentions_Imperfect_Execution_Women_Get_Fewer_of_the_Hot_Jobs_Needed_to_Advance.pdf

"How to Properly Define 'Great Leader'—And Act Like One" by Geoff Smart (July 3, 2012) http://www.fastcompany.com/1841916/3-behaviors-of-great-leaders?partner=rss

"Lack of Self-Promotion Hurts Women in Large Firms" by Patricia Gillette, *The Am Law Daily* (July 7, 2009) http://amlawdaily.typepad.com/amlawdaily/2009/07/self-promotion.html

"Power in Law–Lessons from the 2011 Women's Power Summit on Law and Leadership" Center for Women in Law (January 2012) http://gallery.mailchimp.com/855969b6d5bf3c410aac76f88/files/Summit_White_Paper_FINAL.pdf

"Reinvigorating the Initiative and Celebrating Successful Women: Breaking the Glass Ceiling" *San Francisco Attorney* Magazine (Spring 2010) http://www.sfbar.org/forms/sfam/q12010/no-glass-ceiling-1.pdf

"Report of the Seventh Annual NAWL National Survey on Retention and Promotion of Women in Law Firms" (October 2012) http://nawl.timberlakepublishing.com/files/NAWL%202012%20Survey%20Report%20final.pdf

"Seven Characteristics of Successful Women Leaders" by Lynn Banis, http://ezinearticles.com/?7-Characteristics-of-Successful-Women-Leaders&id=4784705

Study by Pew Research Institute on Who's a Better Leader http://pewresearch.org/pubs/932/men-or-women-whos-the-better-leader

"Top Ten Characteristics of Successful Women Business Leaders" Women's Leadership Exchange http://www.womensleadershipexchange.com/index.php?pagename=resourceinfo&resourcekey=166

"Women at Work" Statistics on the Female Workforce by the Bureau of Labor Statistics http://www.bls.gov/spotlight/2011/women/

"Women in Federal and State-Level Judgeships" Center for Women in Government & Civil Society, Rockefeller College of Public Affairs & Policy, University at Albany, State University of New York (Summer 2012) http://www.albany.edu/womeningov/publications/summer2012_judgeships.pdf

"Women in Law in the U.S." Catalyst (October 2012) http://www.catalyst.org/knowledge/women-law-us

"Women 'Take Care,' Men 'Take Charge': Stereotyping of U.S. Business Leaders Exposed" Catalyst http://www.catalyst.org/publication/94/women-take-care-men-take-charge-stereotyping-of-us-business-leaders-exposed

# Appendix B

## TOOLS

Risk-Taking Profile:
http://newberrycoaching.com/2012/what-is-your-risk-taking-profile/

Leadership Legacy Assessment Test:
http://www.yourleadershiplegacy.com/assessment/assessment.php

Credible Communication Techniques:
http://newberrycoaching.com/2012/is-your-communication-style-undermining-your-credibility/

Leadership Self Test:
http://www.schulersolutions.com/leadership_self_test.html

What Are Your Top Five (how to acknowledge your strengths):
http://newberrycoaching.com/2013/what-are-your-top-five/

Leadership Lever Self-Assessment:
http://newberrycoaching.com/2012/what-leadership-levers-do-you-need-to-pull/

### Author Biography
# Gindi Eckel Vincent

**G**indi Eckel Vincent began practicing her leadership skills at an early age on an audience of dolls, younger siblings and cousins, and neighborhood children that tolerated her "direction." As her style and vision matured, Ms. Vincent's interest in leadership grew through her volunteer efforts in the community and school. Since graduating from Vanderbilt Law School, she has led teams and committees within the private law firms and companies where she worked. Ms. Vincent currently serves as counsel in ExxonMobil's law department. She has over fifteen years of experience as an environmental attorney, previously advising energy companies on complex environmental challenges at Pillsbury Winthrop Shaw Pittman LLP.

In addition to her leadership roles at work, Ms. Vincent has led numerous bar associations and charitable organizations. She served as chair of the board of the 27,000-member Texas Young Lawyers Association, president of the Fort Worth Young Lawyers Association, and chair of the Houston Young Lawyers Foundation. Ms. Vincent also volunteers with numerous charitable and community organizations, including serving as vice president of the Young Audiences of Houston and director of programs for the Women's Energy Network. In 2010, she received both the Working Mother of the Year Award from Pillsbury Winthrop and the Outstanding Young Lawyer of Houston Award. In 2013, the Houston Can Academies selected Ms. Vincent as the recipient of its 2013 Motherhood: The Lifetime Achievement Award.

Ms. Vincent speaks and writes nationally on both legal and non-legal topics, including a daily blog for working women at www.gindivincent.com. She is married to Bray, a rancher and restaurateur, and they live in Houston, Texas, where they are still figuring out life with their three precocious preschoolers—triplets are her biggest leadership challenge to date!

### Advisor Biography
# Mary B. Cranston

**M**ary B. Cranston is the retired senior partner and immediate past chair of Pillsbury Winthrop Shaw Pittman LLP. Pillsbury is an international law firm with over 800 attorneys in fifteen offices, including San Francisco, New York, Washington, D.C., Los Angeles, London, Tokyo, and Shanghai. In her eight years as chair, she expanded the firm from a regional California base into an international platform through two large mergers and the addition of seven offices.

Ms. Cranston is an expert in complex class action litigation, antitrust counseling and litigation, regulated industries counseling and litigation, and securities litigation. She has litigated over 300 class actions in the state and federal courts and is an expert on class action procedural and trial issues and all aspects of class action settlements.

She currently serves on five public company boards: VISA, Juniper Networks, International Rectifier, GrafTech (where she currently serves as lead director), and Exponent. She has also served on numerous nonprofit boards, including Catalyst, the Stanford University Board of Trustees, the San Francisco Ballet, the Commonwealth Club, the Lucile Packard Children's Hospital (where she currently serves as chair), and the Stanford Hospital.

Ms. Cranston has been named one of "The 100 Most Influential Lawyers in America" by the *National Law Journal*, one of two "Best Law Firm Leaders in the United States" by *Of Counsel*, and one of the "Top 100 Lawyers in California" by the *San Francisco Daily Journal* and the *Los Angeles Daily Journal*. She has been profiled as "One of the Best Female Antitrust Lawyers in the World" by *Global Competition Review*. For the past eight years, she has been included in the *San Francisco Business Times* List of the Most Influential Women in Bay Area Business, and in 2004, she received the Athena Award given to the outstanding Bay Area businesswoman for lifetime achievement. In 2005, Ms. Cranston was the recipient of the Margaret Brent Women Lawyers of Achievement Award, the

American Bar Association's highest award for women lawyers given for legal excellence and for paving the way for other women lawyers. In 2010, she was awarded the Stanford Medal by Stanford University for exceptional lifetime contributions to the university. In 2013, she was selected by the *San Francisco Business Times* and the *Silicon Valley Business Times* for their Outstanding Director Award.

# About the ABA Commission on Women in the Profession

As a national voice for women lawyers, the ABA Commission on Women in the Profession forges a new and better profession that ensures that women have equal opportunities for professional growth and advancement commensurate with their male counterparts. It was created in 1987 to assess the status of women in the legal profession and to identify barriers to their advancement. Hillary Rodham Clinton, the first chair of the commission, issued a groundbreaking report in 1988 showing that women lawyers were not advancing at a satisfactory rate.

Now in its third decade, the commission not only reports the challenges that women lawyers face, it also brings about positive change in the legal workplace through such efforts as its Women of Color Research Initiative, Women in Law Leadership Academy, women in-house counsel regional summits, and Margaret Brent Women Lawyers of Achievement Awards. Drawing upon the expertise and diverse backgrounds of its twelve members, who are appointed by the ABA president, the commission develops programs, policies, and publications to advance and assist women in public and private practice, the judiciary, and academia.

For more information, visit www.americanbar.org/women.

# ENDNOTES

1. It's actually ten women in the top 250 Fortune 500 companies (as reported by Rose Hoare, *Meet Fortune 500's female powerbrokers*, CNN May 9, 2012), *available at* http://edition.cnn.com/2012/05/08/business/f500-leading-women.

2. BUREAU OF LABOR STATISTICS, U.S. DEP'T OF LABOR, CURRENT POPULATION SURVEY, ANNUAL AVERAGES 2008, tbl. 1, 2009.

3. Mitra Toossi, *Labor force projections to 2020: a more slowly growing workforce*, MONTHLY LABOR REV., Jan. 2012, at 44, *available at* http://www.bls.gov/opub/mlr/2012/01/art3full.pdf.

4. BUREAU OF LABOR STATISTICS, U.S. DEP'T OF LABOR, WOMEN IN THE LABOR FORCE: A DATABOOK, 2012, *available at* http://www.bls.gov/cps/wlf-databook-2012.pdf.

5. *Projections of Education Statistics by 2016*, tbls. 27-31, NAT'L CTR. FOR EDUC. STATISTICS, http://nces.ed.gov/programs/projections/projections2016/tables.asp#t27 (last visited May 11, 2013).

6. *Women at Work*, BUREAU OF LABOR STATISTICS (Mar. 2011), *available at* http://www.bls.gov/spotlight/2011/women/.

7. Hoare, *supra* note 1 (this is still up a dramatic six women in 2012 over 2011, when only twelve women held the role of CEO in a Fortune 500 company).

8. John Gettings, David Johnson, Borgna Brunner & Chris Frantz, *Wonder Women: Profiles of leading female CEOs and business executives*, INFOPLEASE, *available at* http://www.infoplease.com/spot/womenceo1.html#ixzz1xbcL2zqS (last visited May 11, 2013).

9. Rutgers Center for American Women and Politics, *Women in Elective Office 2013* (Apr. 2013), *available at* http://www.cawp.rutgers.edu/fast_facts/levels_of_office/documents/elective.pdf.

10. Debra Cassens Weiss, *"Gold Standard" Law Firms Named for Placing Women in Leadership; List Could Shrink Next Year*, A.B.A.J. (June 14, 2012, 6:51 A.M.), *available at* http://www.abajournal.com/news/article/gold_standard_law_firms_named_for_placing_women_in_leadership_list_could_sh/.

11. NAFE & Flex-Time Lawyers, *"Executive Summary," Best Law Firms for Women 2011* (2011).

12. A.B.A. COMM'N ON WOMEN, A CURRENT GLANCE AT WOMEN IN THE LAW (Feb. 2013), *available at* http://www.americanbar.org/content/dam/aba/marketing/women/current_glance_statistics_feb2013.pdf.

13. CATALYST, WOMEN IN LAW IN THE U.S. (Mar. 2013), *available at* http://www.catalyst.org/knowledge/women-law-us.

14. Anne-Marie Slaughter, *Why Women Still Can't Have It All*, THE ATLANTIC, July–August 2012.

15. Laurel Bellows, *Shattering the Glass Ceiling: Initiatives Under Way to End Gender Inequity in the Legal Profession*, A.B.A.J., Feb. 2013, *available at* http://www.abajournal.com/magazine/article/lets_shatter_the_glass_ceiling.

16. Wm. T. (Bill) Robinson III, *Advancement of Women Lawyers: Barriers Must Be Removed so Female Attorneys Can Equally Participate*, A.B.A. J., Jan. 1, 2012.

17. Robin Madell, *7 Myths About Getting Ahead—What Women Need To Know*, CAREER-INTELLIGENCE.COM, *available at* http://www.career-intelligence.com/management/Seven-Myths-About-Getting-Ahead.asp (last visited May, 10 2013).

18. CATALYST, WOMEN "TAKE CARE," MEN "TAKE CHARGE": STEREOTYPING OF U.S. BUSINESS LEADERS EXPOSED (2005), *available at* http://www.catalyst.org/knowledge/women-take-care-men-take-charge-stereotyping-us-business-leaders-exposed

19. *Id.*

20. *Id.*

21. *Id.*

22. *The Qualities that Distinguish Women Leaders*, CALIPER https://www.calipercorp.com/portfolio/the-qualities-that-distinguish-women-leaders/.

23. *Female Leaders Are Still Stereotyped*, BLOOMBERG BUSINESSWEEK (Oct. 12, 2010) *available at* http://www.businessweek.com/managing/content/oct2010/ca20101012_599532.htm.

24. JILL FLYNN, KATHRYN HEATH, AND MARY DAVIS HOLT, BREAK YOUR OWN RULES: HOW TO CHANGE THE PATTERNS OF THINKING THAT BLOCK WOMEN'S PATHS TO POWER 4 (2011).

25. *Id.*

26. JOANNA BARSH & SUSIE CRANSTON, HOW REMARKABLE WOMEN LEAD: THE BREAK-THROUGH MODEL FOR WORK AND LIFE (2011).

27. SHARON HADARY & LAURA HENDERSON, HOW WOMEN LEAD: THE 8 ESSENTIAL STRATE-GIES SUCCESSFUL WOMEN KNOW (2012).

28. Flynn, et al., *supra* note 24.

29. Barsh & Cranston, *supra* note 26, at 191.

30. Barsh & Cranston, *supra* note 26, at 219-23.

31. Flynn, et al., *supra* note 24, at 52.

32. BILL GEORGE & PETER SIMS, TRUE NORTH: DISCOVER YOUR AUTHENTIC LEADERSHIP (2007).

33. *Id.*

34. *Id.*

35. *Id.*

36. George & Sims, *supra* note 32.

37. Kathy Caprino, *Mandating Women at the Leadership Table: Why the Time is Now,* FORBES (Mar. 25, 2011, 10:55 A.M.), *available at* http://www.forbes.com/sites/85broads/2011/03/25/mandating-women-at-the-leadership-table-why-the-time-is-now/.

38. Barsh & Cranston, *supra* note 26, at 87-88.

39. Barsh & Cranston, *supra* note 26, at 90-91.

40. Barsh & Cranston, *supra* note 26, at 222.

41. SHERYL SANDBERG, LEAN IN: WOMEN, WORK, AND THE WILL TO LEAD (2013).

42. Barsh & Cranston, *supra* note 26, at 214.

43. Barsh & Cranston, *supra* note 26, at 219–220.

44. Barsh & Cranston, *supra* note 26, at 221.

45. JAMES M. STROCK, SERVE TO LEAD: YOUR TRANSFORMATIONAL 21ST CENTURY LEADERSHIP SYSTEM (2010).

46. Hadary & Henderson, *supra* note 27, at xxvii.

47. Hadary & Henderson, *supra* note 27, at 68.

48. Hadary & Henderson, *supra* note 27, at 17–19.

49. Flynn, et al., *supra* note 24, at 14.

50. Flynn, et al., *supra* note 24, at 42.

51. Barsh & Cranston, *supra* note 26, at 206.

52. Barsh & Cranston, *supra* note 26.

53. Hadary & Henderson, *supra* note 27.

54. Susan M. Heathfield, *Leadership Vision, available at* http://humanresources.about.com/od/leadership/a/leader_vision.htm.

55. John L. Waltman, *Reference for Business: Communication,* http://www.referenceforbusiness.com/management/Bun-Comp/Communication.html.

56. Barsh & Cranston, *supra* note 26, at 134.

57. Susan Liddy, *Were You Born to Be in Charge*, FUTURE WOMEN LEADERS WOMEN'S LEADERSHIP BLOG (Feb. 17, 2010, 3:21 P.M.), *available at* http://blog.futurewomenleaders.net/blog/bid/30692/Were-You-Born-to-Be-in-Charge-4-Traits-of-Women-Leaders.

58. George & Sims, *supra* note 32.

59. CAITLIN FRIEDMAN & KIMBERLY YORIO, THE GIRL'S GUIDE TO BEING A BOSS (WITHOUT BEING A BITCH): VALUABLE LESSONS, SMART SUGGESTIONS, AND TRUE STORIES FOR SUCCEEDING AS THE CHICK-IN-CHARGE (2006)

60. Laurel Bellows, *From the Desk of ABA President Laurel Bellows: Sponsor Your Way Up the Ladder*, Sep. 12, 2012, *available at* http://ms-jd.org/desk-aba-president-laurel-bellows-sponsor-your-way-ladder.

61. Flynn, et al., *supra* note 24, at 98.

62. Barsh & Cranston, *supra* note 26, at 170-71.

63. Hadary & Henderson, *supra* note 27, at 92-93.

64. Hadary & Henderson, *supra* note 27, at 169.

65. BARBARA STANNY, SECRETS OF SIX-FIGURE WOMEN (2004) .

66. Neena Newberry, *Four Key Levers to Manage Your Career and Get Results*, NEWBERRY EXECUTIVE COACHING AND CONSULTING LLC (Mar. 8, 2012), *available at* http://newberry-coaching.com/2012/four-key-levers-to-manage-your-career-and-get-results/.

67. Flynn, et al., *supra* note 24.

68. Hadary & Henderson, *supra* note 27, at 73.

69. LINDA BABCOCK & SARA LASCHEVER, WOMEN DON'T ASK: NEGOTIATION AND THE GENDER DIVIDE (2003)

70. Barsh & Cranston, *supra* note 26, at 222.

71. Stanny, *supra* note 65.

72. Flynn, et al., *supra* note 24, at 62.

73. Flynn, et al., *supra* note 24, at 62.

74. Sandberg, *supra* note 41.

75. Flynn, et al., *supra* note 24, at 16.

76. Flynn, et al., *supra* note 24, at 125.

77. Hadary & Henderson, *supra* note 27, at 24.

78. John Baldoni, *New Year's Resolution for Leaders: Take Better Care of You!*, FORBES (Dec. 26, 2012, 1:39 P.M.), *available at* http://www.forbes.com/sites/johnbaldoni/2012/12/26/new-years-resolution-for-leaders-take-better-care-of-you/.

79. Richard Hamon, *Leadership Skills—Apply Your Leadership Skills to Your Own Life and Take Better Care of Yourself*, EZINE ARTICLES, *available at* http://ezinearticles.com/?Leadership-Skills—Apply-Your-Leadership-Skills-to-Your-Own-Life-and-Take-Better-Care-of-Yourself&id=1012341 (last visited May 11, 2013).

80. Barsh & Cranston, *supra* note 26, at 251.